THE SUNDAY TIMES

Successful Presentation Skills

SECOND EDITION

Andrew Bradbury

KOGAN PAGE | *CREATING SUCCESS*

First published in 1995
Second edition 2000

Kogan Page Limited
120 Pentonville Road
London N1 9JN

The views expressed in this book are those of the author and are not necessarily the same as those of Times Newspapers Ltd.

British Library Cataloguing in Publication Data

A CIP record for this book is available from the British Library.

ISBN 0 7494 3259 4

Typeset by Jean Cussons Typesetting, Diss, Norfolk
Printed and bound in Great Britain by Clays Ltd, St Ives plc

contents

where do you want to go?

do *you* need this book?

How important is it for you and your company that your presentations should be top quality, memorable and effective?

Do you stage your presentations as part of an overall strategy, or just whenever 'it seems like a good idea'?

A favourite business buzzword at the moment is 'differentiation' – that certain something that makes your company more attractive to a potential customer than any of your rivals. Part of the difference will undoubtedly come from things like price, quality, reliability and so on. But this is never the whole story. Customers may be willing to accept higher prices if they also get preferential status or better quality. Conversely, they may be willing to accept lower quality – as long as it is still within certain tolerances and as long as they get a better base price and bigger discounts.

But whatever it is that you are offering as a differentiator, your customers must know about it. They must still be convinced that what *you* are offering, at *your* prices, etc is the best fit for their requirements. In practice, the only way you can really differentiate your company is by making the most effective sales pitch – the most impressive presentation. Yet if many of the presentations I've seen over the years are anything to go by, most of us – from junior salesman to managing director – could derive significant benefits from a crash course in basic presentation skills. And that's just what this book is all about.

Most of the tens of thousands of presentations that are going on at any given moment during any working day are intended to sell a product or service, pass on information, elicit ideas or introduce and develop new skills.

In short, if you *ever* have to deal with other people in *any* kind of business situation, this book has something to offer.

all the world's a stage

Almost any kind of business transaction involves some degree of presentation skill. Guiding a new colleague through the basic office procedures, reporting back to a departmental meeting, or giving the members of the board an overview of a new product – in each situation you will be giving a presentation.

In the first case, you may sit down with that new employee and chat over a few of the key features of the job, while in the second example you might jot down a few notes and even prepare a foil or two. For the presentation to the board you would probably take several days to prepare and rehearse your script, design your visual aids and draft a handout. At a superficial level the three situations may appear quite different, yet at heart they are all the same.

Alternatively, you may be visiting a prospective business partner, sitting round the kitchen table with a cup of coffee while you run through the facts and figures on an A4 pad. But is that really any different from discussing the same facts and figures with half a dozen or a dozen people, using a flipchart or a whiteboard instead of sheets of A4 paper?

the seven basic steps

This book is based on the assumption that the whole process for creating *any* presentation consists of seven basic steps:

1. Decide what you want to achieve.
2. Decide whether a formal presentation is the best way to achieve this objective.
3. If you decide to go ahead with the presentation, decide what form it should take.
4. Prepare a script (in whatever form suits you best).
5. Design and prepare your visual aids and handouts.
6. Rehearse.
7. Do it!

The only guaranteed way to produce a poor presentation is through inadequate preparation. I've seen senior business people give the most appalling presentations – because they refused to learn a few basic skills.

The good news is that I've also been to presentations by people who had no special qualifications other than a willingness to put in the necessary time and effort. And many of those presentations were just great!

A good presentation is no more than effective communication between two or more human beings. There's no mystery about it – unless you've never had the opportunity to find out how to do it right. It is a skill, and like any other skill it can be learnt. The very fact that you are reading this book tells me that you are a person who is willing to learn.

As Chris Sullivan, a senior consultant with Guardian Business Services, explains:

> Even people who look unpromising can draw it out from within themselves. People who stutter and stammer will still stutter and stammer, but they can present effectively in spite of that.

Of course this book won't turn you into a Winston Churchill or a John F Kennedy overnight. Those men, and other men and women like them, have all shared one quality that no book can give you – the *desire to communicate*. That is the one quality only you can provide. It doesn't have to be a desire to speak to nations. You don't even have to plan to address rallies of several hundred people. It is sufficient that you want to make that basic contact with your audience, even when that audience is no more than a man, a boy and a dog, as they say.

presentations are about communication

First and foremost, this book is about *communicating*. It will show you how to understand your audience, and how to relate to them in the most effective manner.

It assumes no prior knowledge, and covers everything you need to know to deliver successful presentations.

By the way, you might want to equip yourself with a pen or highlighter to mark the points that are of special interest to you, points that you particularly want to remember.

Many people find that the very act of underlining or highlighting a piece of information helps them to absorb it more readily. Maybe it would work for you, too?

2, 4, 6, 8 – how do you communicate?

it's not *what* you say

One of the best kept secrets of the business world costs companies vast amounts of money, wastes millions of working hours per year, and can be summed up in two short sentences:

> Most business presentations do not achieve their intended purpose. Worse still, they frequently achieve *nothing* of any value!

Have you ever been in a situation where you felt that you had really presented a very convincing case for or against a certain course of action, yet nobody seemed to be the least bit affected by what you said?

This apparent failure may simply be due to the fact that you were saying something that nobody wanted to hear. It is much more likely, however, that you were placing too much dependence upon the power of your words and your logic, and paying too little attention to other aspects of your very personal contribution to the presentation.

For example, when you are trying to influence other people, how aware are you of your body language, your vocal style and your 'presence' (that vague personal quality also known as 'charm' or 'charisma')? And do you realize that, where there are conflicting messages, the way that these non-verbal qualities are perceived by other people will normally far outweigh the effect of anything you might *say*, be it in an intimate conversation or in a major presentation?

Studies from both Britain and the United States show that we tend to base our judgement of other people on three main characteristics:

- ■ Verbal Content = 7%
- ■ Vocal Interest = 38%
- ■ Body Language = 55%

While the exact percentages may vary slightly, depending on the particular situation, these figures show that at least 90 per cent of your public image depends on *how* you look and sound rather than *what* you actually say.

it's the way that you say it

Not only do we pay close attention to these 'non-verbal' signals, but it also seems that we have quite clear ideas as to what the signals mean. For example, how well do you know your own voice? Is it deep and gruff, about average or a little high pitched? Do you speak quickly, slowly or at a medium pace? Do you have an extensive range of tones and inflections which make your voice interesting to listen to, or (be honest) does your voice tend to become rather monotonous if you have to speak for any length of time (more than four or five minutes of continuous speech, for example)?

The answer you give may explain a lot about the way that other people react to you. A person who speaks slowly and in a lower than average tone is widely perceived as being powerful and credible. Someone with a faster, higher-toned voice will be seen as enthusiastic but lightweight through to positively untrustworthy.

And what about your body language? Here, too, you may be 'saying' a lot more about yourself without ever realizing it.

For example, a person whose gestures are few and far between is seen as being powerful, deliberate and intelligent. The sort of person who makes frequent, expansive gestures may be seen as frivolous or even a couple of sandwiches short of a picnic.

Remember, then, if your overall personal style is inconsistent, your audience will base their impressions on the 93 per cent non-verbal signals you put out rather than the 7 per cent of verbal content, no matter how clever, logical and reasonable that verbal content may be.

I'm really pleased to be here – maybe

Here's a simple example of how this might work in practice:

Imagine that you have been invited to attend the launch of a new product which the manufacturers hope will be a world-beater. After a rather long wait, a door opens and a man enters and walks wearily to the podium set up at the front of the room. He is tall, and well dressed in dark suit, white shirt and discreetly patterned tie. His hair is carefully styled and his shoes look smart, well polished and expensive. He reaches the podium, and waits for a minute or so with shoulders bowed, grasping the sides of the lectern as though his life depended on it. He stares down at his notes and *avoids* establishing eye contact with the audience as he makes his opening remarks in a voice that is tired and monotonous, even depressed:

> Good morning, ladies and gentlemen. May I start by saying how nice it is to see such a large audience. I think I can safely promise you a very interesting and stimulating day…

Do *you* believe that he is pleased to see you? Do *you* believe his promise that the events which are to follow will be interesting and stimulating? Are you looking forward to what is to come – or working out how to make a speedy exit without being too conspicuous?

I suspect that your answers would reflect some very low expectations about this event. Yet this cannot be due to anything that has been *said*. If you take the words out of context, the message they convey is polite, positive and even enthusiastic. But once the verbal content is combined with the incongruent, contradictory vocal signals and body language, it is the signals and body language that we believe, and not the verbal content. Of course this works the other way round, as well.

Some while ago, researchers at the Pepperdine campus of the UCLA ran a series of 'scientific' presentations. What the audiences didn't know was that the speakers were not highly qualified medical people speaking about their latest research. Rather, they were highly skilled actors and actresses delivering carefully prepared nonsense (that is, the scripts contained plenty of appropriate jargon, but really didn't make much sense when studied in detail).

All of the presentations were received with great enthusiasm, right up to the moment when audience members were handed printouts of the speeches and quickly realized that it was all a load of bunk.

It was, in short, an outstanding demonstration of how readily we can be persuaded by a calm, confident, positive manner, even when we should be intellectually aware that the persuader's message is nothing more than a load of hot air.

In short, the most brilliant speech ever written will ultimately depend for its success on the *presentation style* of the *speechmaker* and not on the *contents* of the speech itself.

No matter what the situation, if your *style* of presentation isn't an audience-grabber the *content* begins to become irrelevant. At the worst extreme, a truly unskilled presenter can put his material across in such a way that the members of the audience not only don't take it in, they don't even care that they haven't taken it in. They are just glad when the presentation is over.

A particularly powerful example of this phenomenon at work must be the pre-election debate between John F Kennedy and Richard M Nixon when the two men were competing for the post of President of the United States in 1960.

Those people who only *heard* the debate on radio had to rely on the verbal content and vocal signals to guide their perceptions. Most people in this group regarded Nixon as the better candidate.

Of the people who *saw* the debate on television, and received verbal content and the vocal signals *and* saw the body language of the two speakers, the majority perceived John F Kennedy as being a far more credible candidate.

It is a simple fact of history that it was Nixon who had the policies, but Kennedy who won the presidency!

The presenter who can create rapport with her audience is operating on both the conscious *and* the subconscious levels. At its best the effect can be quite magical. The good news is that there is nothing 'magical' about it. It is a skill which almost anyone can master with a little time and effort.

when you feel the fear...

panic now – and avoid the rush

You're sitting quietly at your desk when suddenly the call comes: 'we need a presentation, and only *you* can do it!' What do you feel? Pride? Caution? Or unadulterated

PANIC

Since most people are likely to opt for *panic*, why not turn this to your advantage by using it as a five-part reminder of the key elements of a good presentation:

Outline your	Purpose
Analyse your	Audience
Identify the	Need
Collate your	Information
Prepare your	Communication

purpose

In many cases the purpose of a presentation will not be a matter of choice – it will be dictated for you by someone else or by the context in which the presentation will take place:

- ■ Your department head asks you to show Sally Gorringe (a new employee) the ropes.
- ■ You are chosen to give senior management a brief overview of the work done by your team.
- ■ It is your task to round out the proceedings at a sales conference in a positive and motivating fashion.

On Monday morning Bob's boss, Mark, called him in and told him that he was going to be doing a presentation on their latest product ('Product X') for the benefit of some customers who would be visiting the company's offices on Thursday afternoon.

On Thursday afternoon Bob waited patiently in the meeting room that had been set aside for his presentation. Eventually, at 4.45 pm, Bob's boss and the eight visitors trooped into the room. With little more than a nod to Bob, Mark showed the visitors to their seats, took his place at the front of the room, said a few words to introduce Bob – and then sat down.

Bob, making the best he could of the situation, gave what he thought was really a pretty good presentation on Product X. He ran through some historical information about why the company had decided to bring this particular product to market. He brought in some background material on the development of Product X, and he rounded things off by announcing the intended preview and release dates for Product X.

The next day, Mark called Bob into his office again, but not to congratulate him.

'What the blue blazes was all that about?' Mark demanded. 'I spent the whole afternoon taking those guys round the factory, showing them how Product X was developed and so on. And when we get to your presentation they have to sit through a cut down version of the same material!

'All I wanted from you was a nice little piece, about ten to fifteen minutes long, to round out everything I'd been saying and to encourage them to place some hefty advance orders!'

In order to produce a successful presentation you must have a clear idea of what the presentation is to be about. Furthermore, your understanding must be both precise and accurate. If necessary, push for further information until you are sure that you have a solid grasp on that purpose:

■ Are you required to train Sally Gorringe in some specific tasks, or simply to familiarize her with the general routine?
■ Are you doing a solo presentation to senior management, or are you one of half a dozen speakers?
■ What are the current sales figures like? Will your own presentation be preceded by rewards or recriminations?

There has been many a good presentation that has fallen by the wayside because the speaker wasn't sufficiently clear about his purpose.

audience

In the examples we've just looked at, a specific audience has been mentioned each time – the new employee, senior management and the sales team.

One of the first things you should do when preparing for any presentation is find out as much as you can about your intended audience, and then focus your presentation accordingly.

Even if you don't have any opportunity to meet any of the

members of your audience in advance, you can still use a simple but surprisingly powerful test to make a pretty accurate estimate.

Q1:   If I'm describing a new idea to you, would you prefer that I start with (a) the details, or (b) the big picture?

Q2a: If you answered (a) to question 1, would you like me to (c) work up from the details to the bigger picture, or (d) stick with the details?

Q2b: If you answered (b) to question 1, would you want me to (e) work down to a more detailed description, or (f) stick with the big picture?

If you answered (a) and (d) you obviously prefer to work with details, whereas someone who selected (b) and (f) is probably much more comfortable dealing in generalities. A person who selects (a) and (c) is primarily detail oriented, but is also interested to see how those details relate to the big picture. Finally, if you selected (b) and (e), then you probably prefer to work in generalities, whilst being able to deal with more precise details when this is appropriate.

We can apply these conclusions to job roles to estimate what kind of presentation style the corresponding job-holders might prefer.

Most senior managers and board members are required to think in terms of company strategy for the next five years, and competition at the national and international level. It seems likely, then, that such people would select answers (b) and limited (e) – indicating a fairly non-detailed type of presentation. Staff in the R&D department, on the other hand, are more likely to answer (a) and (d), which would call for lots of facts and figures in either the presentation or in the supporting handout.

A presentation at a Sales Conference might tend to be (b) and (f) if the main purpose is to celebrate the year's results, or (b) and very limited (e) at the rollout of a new product.

If you're still not sure what approach to adopt, you might try starting with a reasonable degree of detail, working up towards a more general overview. Leave plenty of time for people to ask questions.

need

Every presentation has a *reason*, and *needs*. The *purpose* of taking Sally Gorringe through the office procedures may be to bring her up to speed in her job as quickly as possible, but what are her *needs*? Does she need detailed instructions, or just a brief refresher?

And what do *you* need in order to be able to meet this requirement? Can you 'do it with your eyes shut'? Or do you need to do some research? Is this a routine situation, or a chance to put yourself in line for promotion?

The more clearly you can define the *needs* of the situation, the more chance you have of giving a really 'spot on' presentation.

information

So, you now know who your presentation is for, and why. But what information should be included to achieve the required outcome? If you give too little information the event becomes a waste of everyone's time. Give too much information and most of it will be forgotten by the next day – and the event becomes a waste of everyone's time.

The more accurately you define your goal, the easier it will be to determine what must go into the presentation – and what can be left out.

communication

What visual aids will you use (if any)? Where will the presentation be staged? What kind of follow-up will be required?

This is where you plan the *framework* for your presentation, and consider the all-important question: How will it be perceived by your audience (will they hear what you *meant* to say, what you *did* say, what they *think* you said or what they *think* you *meant* by what they *think* they heard you say)?

your 'performing edge'

It is quite normal to feel some degree of apprehension when you are about to embark on an activity that is both important and, to a certain extent, unknown. Will the audience be responsive? Will your presentation be appropriate to their needs? Will the mains power supply flow smoothly? A presenter who doesn't feel any apprehension before an event is generally, in my experience, not nearly as skilled in delivering presentations as he thinks he is.

The 'secret' remedy for so-called stage fright is simply to acknowledge the feeling without letting it upset you. Trying to ignore those feelings is self-defeating, because you have to keep thinking about the feelings in order to remember what it is you are trying to ignore!

When you feel a little nervous, 'reframe' that feeling. Reinterpret what is happening to you as a process of revving up for a really successful performance. Remind yourself that a little extra adrenalin helps to give you a 'performing edge'. Then concentrate on all the things that you are going to do to make this your best presentation yet.

winning ways

A genuinely effective way to acquire new skills is to find out what acknowledged experts do, understand what makes them successful, and then apply that behaviour in your own life – and thereby learn to duplicate that success.

A major car company was preparing to launch a brand new luxury saloon on to the European market. It was considerably more expensive than any of their existing cars, and they were concerned that they would not be able to find enough people with the kind of sales skills needed to make the launch successful.

At last, in desperation, they called in a specialist who quickly established that there were already two or three people who had the required levels of skill and knowledge.

Though not himself a car salesman, the expert modelled the three top sales people for several weeks until he felt sure that he understood what they were doing which put them head and shoulders above their colleagues.

The specialist set out the key skills, behaviours and techniques in the form of a training programme that was delivered to the rest of the sales force.

Naturally the results were a little variable, and the trainees weren't immediately able to match the skills of their high-flying colleagues. Nevertheless, over 90% of the trainees showed such radical improvement that the launch was able to go ahead as planned, and was reckoned to be a complete success.

The following list sets out the five skills most frequently used by people rated by their colleagues as outstanding presenters:

> Fine-tuning
> Outcomes
> Chunking
> Unlimited points of view
> Success assurance

■ **Fine-tuning**
A skilled presenter constantly hones and refines her material to make it as appropriate as possible for a given audience. This process continues until the very end of the event, and the presenter will repeatedly

check that the presentation is headed in the right direction, using her skill and *flexibility* to adapt the style, tempo and focus of the presentation in order to achieve her original objectives.

■ **Achieving outcomes**
If you don't know where you want to go, how will you know which route to take? And how will you know when you've arrived? Top presenters work to answer two basic questions right from the start of the planning stage:
– What do I want the presentation to achieve?
– How will the audience behave if I am achieving my outcome?

■ **Effective chunking**
'Chunking' is an essential skill which might be described as 'the process of presenting information in manageable segments'. Some people like to start with an overview and work down to the nitty-gritty, and others will prefer to start with the details and build up to the big picture.

Skilled presenters most frequently *chunk* downwards. That is to say, they start with an overview and work down to the details. They also watch for audience reactions which will tell them if they are working in the right direction and at the right pace.

■ **Unlimited points of view**
Many top speakers give their presentations from *three* different positions: Position 1 is their own viewpoint, Position 2 is the audience's viewpoint, and Position 3 is the 'neutral observer' or 'fly on the wall' position.

By mentally switching from one position to another they can give their presentation a personal dimension (Position 1), they can judge how they are coming across to the audience (Position 2), and can avoid any conflict or confrontation, should it arise, by moving to Position 3.

This particular skill takes time to develop, but it is an amazingly effective key to handling any kind of audience and any kind of situation.

■ **What *must* be, *will* be**

The fifth characteristic common to most skilful presenters is an unshakeable belief that each presentation is bound to be successful, no matter what happens. It is as though they are saying to themselves, albeit quite unconsciously: 'This is the outcome I *require* – therefore it *will* occur.'

it must be seen to be believed

Before you read on, recall an incident from your past that is associated with very strong *positive* emotions – winning a prize, the first time you fell in love or whatever. Remember as much as you can about the event. Bring to mind the sights, sounds, physical feelings and so on. Then come back to the present and take stock of your state of mind.

How do you feel now? Probably a lot better than when you started to read this section. Yet nothing actually happened. Your emotional reactions were triggered by a memory, not by an actual event.

You have just demonstrated a very simple form of the technique known as *visualization*, and its power to generate positive emotions.

Visualization can also be used to focus your efforts more effectively by creating a mental image of a desired event as *though it had already happened*! There is nothing magical about the process, it is based on a simple psychological fact:

The 'middle' or *emotional brain* cannot tell the difference between an actual experience and a fictional event, be it read, heard, seen or imagined.

Effective visualization is simply a way of convincing our middle brain that something imagined is, in fact, real. The more vividly we imagine the event, the more the middle brain is convinced that the event must be real – and stores it as *a remembered fact*!

the pudding of proof

Please understand that visualization is unlikely to work if you try to convince yourself about something you don't really believe is possible. For the best results, set yourself realistic goals and build upon them as your belief grows.

Concentrate on your own actions and feelings. As a daily activity, build up an increasingly detailed mental image of yourself delivering the presentation in a confident and effective manner.

Tell yourself that you are going to do the best job you can on this presentation, that you are going to be successful, and that you *deserve* that success. You will be amazed at the strength of belief in yourself which develops when you regularly practise this technique.

By the way, you will find that your visualization is even more effective if you can spend some time in the room where the presentation will take place. If it is at all possible, do take the opportunity to get the 'feel' of the room – its size, the level of any background noise, the seating layout and so on. Stroll around the room as though you owned the place. Do whatever it takes to make your visualization as realistic as it can be.

Focus your attention on generating positive images and feelings about your role in the presentation. If the whole visualization process seems a bit strange at first, go with it, this is perfectly normal and won't prevent you from achieving a beneficial result. After only a few days you will begin to notice changes in your attitude to the presentation, and before long you'll actually be looking forward to it.

pictures and images

Before reading this next section, please close your eyes and imagine relaxing on a beautiful sandy beach. Take particular note of the first thing that comes to mind.

Now, what was that first thought? Was it a picture, of silver sand, gentle waves on the sea, a clear blue sky or whatever? Was it a sound, of waves splashing gently on the shore, perhaps? Or was it a feeling, of fine sand beneath your feet or the warmth of the sun on your body, for example?

If the first thought was some kind of picture then your primary thinking style (PTS) in this context is *visual*. If your first thought was of something you could hear then your PTS for this experience is *auditory*. And if your first thought was about how you felt (either physically or emotionally), then your PTS is *kinaesthetic*.

> **Note:** Some people may find that they use two PTSs more or less simultaneously. This is often the case, and, for the purposes of the discussion which follows, those two PTSs should be regarded as equal in importance.

In the last couple of sections I've deliberately referred to mental *images* rather than mental *pictures*. People often think that 'visualization' has to be based on literally seeing pictures in your mind. This is not, in fact, correct.

For reasons explained elsewhere in this book (see the beginning of Chapter 10, for example), visual images are a particularly powerful way of conveying ideas. But we don't all have the 'visual filter' as our PTS, and calling up mental pictures is easier for some people than for others.

In practice your visualization should be based on whichever PTS(s) came first when you did the exercise at the start of this section (the PTS(s) which for you is/are associated with pleasure and relaxation). In this context, a visualization based primarily on sound or feelings will work just as well as one based on pictures. What matters is simply that you use the PTS(s) which is/are most natural for you.

confidence matters

you're never alone in a presentation – it just feels like that

Are you a good letter writer? Do you feel comfortable dealing with people over the phone?

If you answered 'yes' to either of these questions you have already learnt to deal with the presenter's Number One nightmare: *lack of feedback*.

In a face-to-face conversation we are provided with a stream of almost instantaneous signals, both verbal and non-verbal, which let us know how the other person or people in the conversation feel about what we are saying.

During a telephone conversation the *physical* non-verbal signals are entirely absent, and we must take our cues from the other person's tone of voice and choice of words. Given that many people have a quite distinct 'telephone manner', even these verbal signals aren't always entirely reliable, however, and this is one of the main reasons why some people prefer not to deal with important and sensitive matters over the phone.

When it comes to writing a letter we get no feedback whatever, of course, which is why so many adults tend to write letters that are nearly as clipped and brief as a telegram.

Delivering a presentation – in terms of the feedback received – ranks somewhere between making a phone call and writing a letter. And that's important, because surveys have shown that most people tend to treat no feedback as *negative feedback*!

Yet there is absolutely no reason why this should be the case.

Martin is giving a presentation at his company's head office. He starts badly, fussing with his OHP foils and vainly trying to get the projected image 'squared up' on the screen. He is clearly ill at ease, and his opening remarks are liberally peppered with 'ers', 'ums' and 'ahs'.

Then, after the first few minutes, the presentation suddenly begins to improve quite noticeably in pace and clarity. Martin has somehow overcome his initial nervousness and is now in full control of the event.

The only feature of the latter portion of Martin's presentation that seemed a little strange was the fact that he looked so long and so frequently towards one particular section of the audience.

---

across a crowded room

So what miracle saved Martin's presentation from disaster?

No miracle. Martin simply found a friendly face, someone who was leaning forward in their seat, who appeared to be concentrating on every word he said, and who laughed at his humorous asides.

The poor start was primarily due to Martin's feelings of isolation, of being 'on the spot'. He allowed his negative feelings to take the upper hand and showed his lack of confidence. The audience picked up on these non-verbal messages and their body language reflected their own negative feelings. It was very fortunate that Martin kept his wits about him so that, when he did find a friendly face, he was able to establish a positive rapport with that member of the audience. From that point on, he was able to pull himself back from the brink of disaster and deliver a satisfactory presentation.

It's true, then: we aren't really cut off from any kind of feedback when we give a presentation after all – it just feels like that. The real problem is that we get relatively little feedback, and what we do get is of a type that we seldom if ever consciously recognize, namely '*non*-verbal signals'.

that certain look

Imagine that you are giving a presentation right this minute. You look out at your audience and you notice a woman in her mid- to late thirties, sitting slightly to your right, has her left leg crossed comfortably over the right so that the left knee is pointing more or less in your direction. Her head is tilted slightly to her right and upwards. Her right hand is resting against her cheek, with the fingers loosely closed, except the index finger, which is pointing straight upwards.

Now, if I say that the woman is looking bright and interested, it won't take much thought to realize that the woman's attitude is positive. But we can actually interpret the meaning of this set (or *cluster*) of body signals much more precisely than that.

The woman's overall deportment is signalling interest and approval. Crossed legs, with the upper knee towards someone, generally indicates interest in that person (the crossed leg position is only negative when the legs are firmly 'locked'). The hand-to-face gesture is also a sign of positive evaluation, as long as the head is not being supported and the mouth is not covered. The head slightly tilted to one side is another indication of interest, as compared to the downward tilted head, which is associated with a negative or critical attitude. The cluster as a whole (and body language must be taken 'as a whole' to have any chance of arriving at an accurate interpretation) says that this member of the audience is on your side, you 'share the same language'.

When you look out at your audience, far from giving you no feedback, they are actually sending you a whole host of messages if only you can recognize them.

Nor do you need to become an expert in reading body language in order to use it as a confidence booster. The only gestures that are worth spotting, in this context, are the positive ones. Like Martin you should look out for the friendly, approving, interested members of your audience, then work to increase the rapport between those people and yourself. As the enthusiasm builds, because of the *Aura Effect* (see Chapter 14) other members of the audience will find it hard not to become involved.

Of course, body language is not an infallible guide to understanding human behaviour. If someone seems to be half asleep during a presentation it could be just because they had a late night. A person who spends their time apparently doodling and who never looks up during the entire presentation may actually be taking notes in some form of shorthand or speed writing.

Make it a habit to always look for the most positive interpretation of any audience behaviour, however odd, or even bizarre, it may be at times. This won't always be easy of course, but you really need to aim to be able to generate confidence from within, rather than depending upon the audience to help you out. And for that you need to *be* confident.

ready, willing and able

In practice you would be well advised to start working on any presentation as soon as you have a clear idea of what is required.

Even if you are rerunning a previously delivered presentation, check through your materials.

Are your visual aids as clear and interesting as they could be? Have any of the 'facts' in the presentation changed since you last delivered it? Is there anything you can add, remove or alter to make the presentation more interesting, more useful or more appropriate to the next audience?

To have prepared your presentation as fully as possible, with a tightly edited script, sufficient visual aids and plenty of rehearsal time, is a tremendous confidence builder. It will give you a sense of being in control of your material that you can never get from trying to do everything at the last moment.

a sense of perspective

A second key confidence builder is having a realistic appreciation of your *current* strengths.

Decide what kind of presentation you are capable of delivering. Are you happy about working with a flipchart, or do you prefer to use previously prepared foils on an overhead projector? Do you need to work from some kind of cue cards or script, or are you comfortable speaking without notes? If possible have a chat with someone else in the company whom you regard as being a capable or even talented presenter, and don't be too polite to pick his or her brains.

Finally, when you think you know your own capabilities, try to aim just a bit higher. According to a detailed study carried out some years ago, the average person is successful in approximately 95 per cent of the tasks they undertake. The biggest single cause of failure is not having tried in the first place!

the look, the feel, the sound

We all process our views of the world through a series of filters – audio, visual and sensory. For example, when we are having something explained to us we might say 'That *sounds* OK to me', or 'Now I *see* what you're getting at' or 'That *strikes* me as a good idea'. We unconsciously select our words to express the way we're thinking – our preferred thinking style (PTS) – and we respond most positively to people who seem to be using the same filter(s) that we prefer to use, a case of 'seeing eye to eye', 'being in tune' or 'having certain feelings in common'.

A presenter who only uses the phraseology of his own preferred thinking style may be creating rapport with as few as one-third of the members of his audience. The other two-thirds, though they may never know why, are likely to feel 'out of tune' with the presenter, won't share his 'point of view', or may simply not be able to 'grasp' the meaning of what is being said.

hand signals should be observed

People frequently make small but easily discernible movements that effectively 'point out' their preferred thinking style at that particular moment in time. For example:

■ Rubbing or pointing to the area around the eyes indicates a *visual* PTS. That person probably 'doesn't *see* what you're getting at'. Or perhaps they have '*spotted*' something in one of your OHP foils that '*looks* rather interesting'.

■ Any noticeable movement around the ears *or* the mouth indicates an *audio* PTS at work. For example, if someone starts pulling at their earlobe, this may

      indicate that they don't 'like what they *hear*', but on
      the other hand, they may be thinking that 'there's a lot
      in what you *say*'.

■ Gestures with the arms and/or hands (such as rubbing
      an arm or a leg, or unnecessary adjustments to items of
      clothing) usually accompany a *sensory* response. That
      person may '*feel* that the point you have just made
      needs fleshing out', or they may think that your ideas
      have given them 'something to get to *grips* with'.

As to whether a particular gesture should be interpreted as a
sign of approval or dissent, the expression on the person's face
should make that clear for you.

turning theory into practice

Understanding your audience is yet another source of confidence – knowing both *who* will be attending the presentation,
and, just as importantly, *why*?

A few months ago I went on a tour of the UK with two of my
colleagues, giving presentations on a new piece of software.
Over a period of three months we did the same presentations
nearly two dozen times, from Bristol to Edinburgh, from
Cardiff to London. Moreover, we didn't meet a single delegate
before the moment when they first came through the door of
the presentation room. So how on earth did we ever manage to
analyse our audience?

The first thing we knew was that our audiences would be
very mixed in the ways that the delegates would process the
information we were giving them. That is to say, we knew that
our presentations had to consist of a fairly even mix of auditory, visual and kinaesthetic material. In order to adequately
inform our audiences about the new software we had to *tell*
them what it did, we had to *show* them what it looked like.

Then we had to give them time for some '*hands on*' practical experience so that they *felt comfortable* with it and would take a positive message back to their companies.

We also used the three styles in the very words we used to present our information, so that they could '*hear* what was on offer', '*see* what we meant', and '*grasp* the basic concepts that *underpinned* the design of the new software'.

focused motivation

Another important consideration was how to motivate delegates to buy in to using this new software – which constituted a major change from their previously paper-based procedures.

Contrary to what some books might have you believe, there is no one way to motivate an entire audience. On the contrary, it is much more realistic to think of motivation in terms of a sliding scale between two basic viewpoints, such as *towards* and *away from*, for example.

In very basic terms, when people are in *towards* mode they are motivated by what they can *achieve*. When people are in *away from* mode they are mainly concerned with the things they want to avoid. (The average split in a typical business audience is about 40 per cent *towards*, 40 per cent *away from*, and 20 per cent somewhere in between.)

In this particular case, we knew that many companies were adopting the new software mainly through a fear of losing out if they didn't accept the new practices – a mainly *away from* way of looking at the situation. We weren't dealing with the companies, however, but with individual end-users – whose personal views might be quite different from those of their company.

On this basis we were careful to cover both sides of the story; the potential dangers of not taking on the new software, and also the many potential benefits that computerization would bring.

the question behind the question

Making this distinction was especially useful when it came to the question and answer sessions. Instead of adopting a sort of middle-of-the-road approach to every question, we could answer each questioner in their own style, and add a little rider at the end of each answer to cater for people with the opposite style.

So, one question that came up several times, in one form or another, went something like this:

> Isn't this going to involve a whole extra learning curve for the people who have to use the software?

Phrased in this way, the question contains the implication that there is something (extra learning) that the questioner would rather not have to deal with (ie *away from* thinking). To meet the questioner on their own ground our answer is, therefore, mainly *away from*, with an element of *towards*:

> Yes, there certainly will be a learning curve, though it is unlikely to be anything like as steep as some people might imagine. [Since the 'someone' is not specifically identified, this sentence will assure *everyone* in the audience that the learning curve won't be as steep as they expect].

> The alternative option [*away from* people don't usually like having options, so this is a double whammy for them] is to carry on with your current methods and get left behind by the companies who do adopt this new way of working. And we all know what getting left behind can mean these days – a fall off in business, downsizing and so on.

> Of course the good news is that companies who accept the need for an extra investment in time and training can expect to see substantial returns on that investment!

Note: Handling audience questions is dealt with in detail in Chapter 13.

the main objective

is this really necessary?

Not long ago I attended a two-hour presentation for about 60 people, staged by a team of four presenters. The whole event must have taken about 170 hours to prepare and deliver – that's *4.8 working weeks*!

And was it worth it? No. It was poorly structured and over detailed. The core information could have been presented far more effectively as a four or five page memo.

So, always start your preparations by asking yourself: 'Is a presentation the *best* way of achieving the required objective?' Check it against the following indicators:

- Do people need to be able to discuss the topic of the presentation in order to reach a decision?
- Do people need to be able to question the presenter in order to fully understand the material?
- Is the presentation designed to 'sell' an idea, a product or a course of action?
- Is there any kind of practical element in the presentation?

If there is no obvious need to deliver information in person then staging a presentation may only be a second best solution.

Roy was asked to prepare a presentation for some of the senior managers. Unfortunately, he was already under pressure to wrap up an existing assignment, and the time needed to prepare and deliver the presentation could seriously jeopardize the chances of meeting the deadline for the current project. Roy decided to review the situation and examine the *real* goal that he was being asked to achieve, which was simply to disseminate information.

Instead of preparing a speech, Roy drew up a wholly adequate *written* description of the required information including half a dozen relevant charts and diagrams. The whole package was put together in a couple evenings, typed up during the day – whilst Roy was getting on with his other work – and was delivered to head office a couple of days ahead of the date of the now defunct presentation.

He didn't waste time turning hard facts into a speech, or rehearsing, or preparing visual aids. Nor did he have to be out of the office for a whole day when time was at a premium. The senior managers also benefited in that they were able to review the material at their leisure and didn't have to put off any last minute appointments that would have clashed with the presentation.

So never *assume* that a presentation is the only way or the best way to communicate information until you've considered all the other options.

and the point is?

If you do decide that a presentation is necessary, there are at least five or six alternative formats, depending on what you want to achieve. To decide which is most appropriate, it helps to start by drawing up a description of your primary objective *in just one sentence*, as shown in the following examples.

The main point of this presentation is to:

- inform all the members of the project as to the current state of play;
- convince senior management that the flexitime system should be extended to include *all* office staff;
- explain why the current production targets are unattainable, and to present a more realistic set of figures;
- motivate the sales force to get behind the company's new product lines.

Give this definition of your primary objective some hard thought, and don't go on until you are satisfied that it is as precise and accurate as you can make it. Then stick to it.

Once you know what you aim to say, you are ready to determine what the presentation is meant to achieve. For example:

- to gather people's views – on a new product, on moves to reshape the company, or whatever;
- to make people aware of an idea or to describe a business opportunity – to gain support for some course of action, or to indicate that action will be required in the future;
- to sell something or to persuade people to take a course of action which they might not wish to take;
- to highlight a problem – to seek a solution, or at least to minimize the effect of the problem;
- to pass on information – to report progress or promote awareness (without requiring any kind of response);
- in education or training – to enhance productivity, encourage a more productive/flexible/efficient work ethic.

Now we need to set out the expected/required *result* of the presentation as clearly as possible.

hold that thought

No matter *why* we want to gather people's opinions on any topic, there are certain basic targets that must be set:

- Everyone involved must clearly understand the nature of the presentation.
- Everyone must understand what input is expected from them.
- It is usually more productive in this kind of presentation to have a medium to high degree of audience interaction – to have people build on each other's ideas.
- The presenter(s) must have some kind of yardstick so that they can tell when the presentation has achieved its goals (or at least has gone as far as it can usefully go).

The basic framework for such a presentation might look something like this:

- Introduce the presentation – motivate the audience.
- Describe what is to be discussed, why, and the required objective(s).
- Open the topic up to discussion.
- Summarize the outcome of the discussion.
- If appropriate, give some indication of the likely outcome of the presentation.

I have a dream

When presenting a new idea, your main objectives may be:

- to have the members of the audience clearly understand the new idea;

- to gain acceptance for the new idea;
- to obtain a commitment to implement the new idea.

In order to achieve these goals the basic outline of your presentation might look something like this:

- Introduce the presentation giving some idea of its purpose – including the need for decision and commitment.
- Describe the *need* for the new idea – does it represent sequential progress or diversification?
- Describe the idea.
- Describe the results and benefits which might reasonably follow the adoption of the new idea.
- Summarize the main points of your presentation and give clear guidelines on what people should do to support the new idea.

roll up, roll up!

In a sense *all* presentations are a form of selling – selling information, ideas, solutions and so on. In a deliberately *persuasive* presentation you will need to include some or all of the following elements:

- The members of the audience must understand what is being asked of them.
- They must accept the need for the proposed action.
- Regardless of whether the audience accepts every word of the arguments you are putting forward, they must be persuaded to *act* in the required manner.

This is potentially the most difficult kind of presentation and must be handled with tact. Nevertheless, a carefully (and correctly) structured presentation can anticipate any negative reactions and actively encourage your audience to 'buy in' to the proposed action rather than fighting against it:

- ■ Introduction. Briefly identify the subject of the presentation, with strong emphasis on any common interests that may be involved – to keep the business running, to reduce costs, and so on.
- ■ Explain why *any* action needs to be taken. Be as frank and as open as possible. And if certain information needs to be withheld to protect the company's commercial interests, then say so.
- ■ Explain exactly what action needs to be taken, and by whom, showing (if possible) how you have reduced any negative element(s) to a minimum.
- ■ Emphasize the *positive* elements of the course of action.
- ■ Summarize the contents of your presentation and call for agreement on the proposals.

no problem too great

When the key element of a presentation relates to a problem, we might approach it in one of three ways, depending on what we have to say about the problem, and what action (if any) we want from other people:

- ■ highlight the problem as a matter of information;
- ■ open the topic up for discussion and possible solutions; or
- ■ offer a solution to the problem, for further discussion.

In each case our primary aim must be to foster understanding of the problem, and in the last two examples we would also want to:

- discuss the pros and cons of the possible solutions;
- gain agreement on what should be done about the problem/solution(s).

The presentation might contain the following elements:

- Introduction. Make it clear whether the presentation is intended simply to highlight the problem, or do you expect some kind of response from the audience?
- Define the problem (including all relevant background and 'historical' information).
- Describe *significant* effects of the problem – who and/or what it affects, how the problem makes itself felt, etc.
- What possible/probable consequences may arise from
  - leaving the problem alone?
  - attacking it?

As appropriate:

- Call for suggestions.
- Describe solution(s).
- Recommend preferred solution (and say why it is preferred).
- Call for decision as to which solution is to be implemented/what further action is to be taken.
- Summarize the main points of the presentation and the discussion, and (where a decision has been reached) indicate what further action will be taken.

now hear this

The final type of presentation is one designed simply to pass on information – to report progress in a certain area of the company's activities, or just promote general awareness.

Just as all presentations require a degree of salesmanship, they also aim to communicate some kind of information. In this particular type of presentation, however, this is the *primary* aim, with no secondary purpose. The presentation will normally contain the following elements:

■ Introduction. Explain what the presentation is about, and what the members of the audience are expected to get out of it.

■ Background information that will give the new material a context that makes sense to the audience. This will make the presentation more enjoyable and the new information more memorable.

■ A clear and simple description of the new information to provide the framework that will make it as easy as possible for the audience to accept and absorb the data.

■ A second review of the information, but this time with supporting evidence/details such as:
   - facts;
   - examples (as close as possible to the audience's area of experience);
   - comparisons;
   - statistics (but keep them simple);
   - expert opinions (where appropriate).

■ Summarize the information, showing how it affects the members of the audience. If the company is moving into new markets, will this mean more work? More money? Greater job security? Show the *whole* picture.

cutting your cloth

These five presentation outlines are designed to:

■ gather opinions;

- ■ publicize an idea or situation;
- ■ sell an idea or course of action;
- ■ highlight a problem (and seek a solution);
- ■ pass on information.

They should be treated as simple templates which can be adapted to fit particular needs and situations. Feel free to pull them about and change them round. Always aim to create presentations in a way that will meet the needs of your audience and which you feel comfortable with. When you feel that a presentation is really *yours*, that's when your audience will perceive that you are in control of your material. This in turn will make them more inclined to accept whatever ideas, plans or information you set before them.

As a practical exercise you might want to scan through the chapter again with the following thought in mind:

Vivian has been asked to do a presentation on a new business opportunity, including a training element, so that members of staff can start to work on it within the next few days.

- ■ What elements should she include in her presentation?
- ■ Should the material be split into two separate presentations?
- ■ What would you do?
- ■ What factors would influence your decision?

---

know your audience

putting the customer first

If there was ever a time for 'putting the customer first', it *must* be when you are preparing a presentation.

Ken, from R&D, has to brief the sales team on any new products which his company plans to bring on to the market. Ken hates doing presentations and keeps them as short as possible. He makes very few notes and gets one of the secretaries to make up his foils.

The foils are so detailed they are unreadable from more than three feet away. Nevertheless, Ken shows each foil for about 20 seconds (with a brief, jargon-laden explanation of each), there are *no* handouts, and Ken refuses to take questions.

Strictly speaking, Ken does include all of the information that the sales team needs to know about the new products. However, as exercises in communication, his briefings are a total flop. Why? Because Ken hasn't given a second's thought for the people he is supposed to be communicating *with*. The sales people would be better off with an audiotape and copies of the foils.

To stage a good presentation it is vital that you concentrate on the basic characteristics of your audience:

- ■ Who will be attending the presentation, and what is their level of seniority/importance?
- ■ Who is the decision maker (where relevant)?
- ■ Is there any point in giving the presentation if certain people are unable to attend?
- ■ Will people be attending your presentation by choice?
- ■ Is their initial attitude likely to be pro, neutral or anti?
- ■ How intelligent are they? *Never* talk down to people.
- ■ How well informed are they? Will they have any background knowledge at all and, if so, how much?
- ■ Will they understand any jargon you normally use?
- ■ What sort of mood will they be in?
- ■ What will they be expecting from you?
- ■ How can you present your material so as to encourage a positive response (and avoid a negative reaction)?

Every time you can accurately gauge one of these factors, and tailor your presentation accordingly, so your communication will be that much more effective.

will they hear what you mean?

Do people automatically understand every word you say? No such luck!

In real life there is always a 'communication gap' – the difference between what I *meant* to say, what I *actually* said, what you *think* you heard and what you *think* I meant.

This gap is particularly important when you are delivering a presentation. After all, the word 'audience' is a *collective* noun.

It appears to be singular, but it is actually shorthand for 'an audience of individual listeners'.

And not just individuals, but individuals who have a wide variety of views on just about any topic you care to mention.

The communication gap

Let me take a moment to give a practical illustration of this point:

Yesterday I watched a child playing with a dog.

What could be more straightforward than this simple sentence? The moment you read those words you understood exactly what they meant – didn't you? Are you sure about that?

See how well *you* can decode the sentence by answering these questions:

- ■ Was the child a little boy or a little girl?
- ■ What age was the child?
- ■ Where did this event take place?
- ■ At what time of day did the event occur?

- What type of dog was the child playing with?
- What colour was the dog?
- Was the dog happy to play with the child?
- Why was I watching the child and the dog – was it my child, or my dog, or both, or neither?

Although we can usually communicate quite easily without cross-checking every word, phrase and sentence, this example shows how much we take language for granted.

As Michael McCasky wrote in the November/December 1979 issue of the *Harvard Business Review*:

Another major point about the verbal environment of managers is that words are symbols, the meanings of which can vary greatly depending on who is using them. The point is troublesome, because it seems so obvious and at the same time contradicts an assumption we usually make in our everyday behavior. I have talked with managers who assume that words are entities and that communicating with another is essentially a process of logically ordering those entities. They direct all their effort toward getting the words right and presenting a logically structured train of thought in order to persuade.

As you examine misunderstandings between two managers, you will often find that what fouls the channels of communication is their mutual assumption that they are using the same words to mean the same things.

vague and precise language

However, if language can be so imprecise, knowing how to use it skilfully – knowing when to be vague and when to be precise, and how to do this without making it painfully obvious to your audience – can be a valuable addition to any presenter's 'toolkit'.

Five of the key factors which identify 'vague' language are:

- ■ **Undefined nouns**
  What is missing in this undertaking: 'If necessary we will provide transport'? What's missing is a definition of the word 'transport'. Does it mean a hire car, a lorry, a bicycle or a pogo stick?

- ■ **Undefined verbs**
  The same principle applies if you get an instruction such as: 'We want you to come to London.' *How* are you supposed to 'come to London'? By plane, by train, by car or on foot? And, incidentally, who will be paying for this trip?

- ■ **Undefined comparisons**
  'Our new product is bigger and better.' But 'bigger' and 'better' than what? Even the apparently more precise 'Our new product is now the best on the market' leaves several important questions unanswered: 'best' as measured by what criteria? What market, precisely? And so on.

- ■ **Unsubstantiated rules**
  'We have to do it this way.' Why, just because you've always done it that way before? What will happen if you use a different approach? Does it have to be done 'this way' even if 'this way' doesn't work?

- ■ **Unattributed quotes**
  'All the research shows…'; 'There was a study that came out last year…'. Who were these researchers? Who did the study, and working to what guidelines? Was the research really directly related to the area being discussed?

It is all too easy to attach our own meanings to other people's words and then assume that they actually meant what we think they meant. This makes it especially important that we do whatever we can to make sure that when we're answering questions, we really understand what is being asked of us.

You may also want to check your own scripts or notes to see whether the degree of precision in your language is appropriate to your purpose.

In some situations, such as technical training, you may want to be very clear about what you mean. A sentence such as:

> Then you take the one you've got left and put it over by the one you did earlier.

Although perfectly clear in your own mind, is unlikely to convey the same meaning to your audience as:

> Then, with both hands, carefully lift the red and black tube, with the cap pointing up so no liquid can leak out, and place it in the empty slot immediately to the left of the green and white striped tube that we prepared in the last session this morning.

If, on the other hand, you wanted to encourage some creativity on the part of your audience – when solving a problem in a team building exercise or brainstorming a name for a new product, for example – then you might deliberately make your language as vague as possible when describing the assignment, in order to give full rein to their powers of imagination.

four learning styles

Every presentation involves some degree of learning, and while you cannot test for the learning mode of every person in the audience, you can at least be aware of, and work to, the four basic learning styles:

- ■ The Tortoise – who likes a strong theoretical basis.
- ■ The Philosopher – who learns from practical evidence.

- ■ The Hare – who prefers to learn from hands-on experience.
- ■ The Entrepreneur – who isn't interested in anything but the bare facts.

The four learning styles can best be understood through various aspects of the overall personality, described here in terms of personal style, typical attitude to life (the motto), how to establish rapport, and what they look for in a presentation.

The Tortoise	The Philosopher
Personal Style: Slow but interesting speech Slow moving but *not* slow witted Avoids eye contact, seldom speaks out voluntarily Tries to fit all new information into existing knowledge base	**Personal Style:** Slow speech with very little variation in tone of voice or facial expression Avoids eye contact Rigid posture Unlikely to speak out, even to ask for clarification
Motto: Today is merely an extension of yesterday	**Motto:** The world would be a far better place if it weren't for the people
To Create Rapport: Speak fairly slowly Don't try to make eye contact Smile a lot (but be sure it is genuine)	**To Create Rapport:** Speak fairly slowly Avoid making eye contact, gesturing or animated speech Show respect for high standards
Presentation Style: Clear, logical structure 'Chunk up' – build up from first principles Support statements with examples and anecdotal evidence	**Presentation Style:** 'Chunk up' – using well-researched, accurate facts Use plenty of examples and anecdotal evidence Give demonstrations wherever possible (and appropriate)

The Hare	The Entrepreneur
Personal Style: Speech is fast and forceful but carefully controlled (may be monotonous) May appear loud and abrupt, even aggressive Maintains prolonged eye contact Formal, self-contained posture	**Personal Style:** Can become obsessed with 'The BIG Picture' Direct, even forceful, but *not* aggressive Enthusiastic and warm approach to life and people
Motto: Anyone still working at 40 is a failure	**Motto:** If it works, it's good, if it doesn't – move on
To Create Rapport: Speak fairly rapidly, using direct, uncomplicated language Maintain steady eye contact At all costs avoid 'chit chat'	**To Create Rapport:** Speak quickly, using colourful language and anecdotes Vary your tone of voice and adopt an upbeat attitude Be energetic and enthusiastic Always address an entrepreneur by name
Presentation Style: Be brief and succinct 'Chunk down' – give the overall view and a few well-chosen facts Support statements with facts, data and statistics	**Presentation Style:** 'Chunk down' – avoiding all unnecessary details Try to find something unusual about the topic Present in an enthusiastic and lively manner Illustrate your points with examples and stories

audiences have feelings, too

It is always useful, as you prepare a presentation, to consider how it will come across to your audience by asking yourself how they might answer the following questions:

- ■ Did you feel that you were being *coerced* or *persuaded*?
- ■ Did you feel that you were being *guided*, or *manipulated*?
- ■ Did you feel *motivated, passive,* or even *uninvolved*?
- ■ Did the presenter successfully create rapport with the audience?
- ■ Did you feel that there was *any* kind of interaction between the presenter and yourself?
- ■ Did you feel that the presenter gave too much or too little *information*, or just the right amount?
- ■ Was there an adequate opportunity to ask questions?
- ■ Did members of the audience get full and relevant answers to their questions?

Only when you are sure that you have addressed these considerations satisfactorily can you begin to feel that you have produced an effective presentation.

Incidentally, when it comes to modelling other presenters, this is a good basic checklist of things to look out for, taking account not only of *what* the presenter does, but also *how* they do it.

words, words, words

more than a licence to talk

According to various studies, we can effectively recall:

- 20% of what we hear;
- 30% of what we see;
- 50% of what we hear *and* see;
- 70% of what we do.

The message is clear: to be truly effective an event must allow the audience to see, and hear and interact with the presenter and the presentation material. In practical terms a presentation must:

- *tell them* what they *need* to know;
- *show them* as much as is necessary to clarify, support and enhance your verbal message;
- create opportunities for *interaction* – and that means more than just allowing time for questions.

Some people find that they can work on all three elements of a presentation at the same time, while others find it easier to write the text, then design the visual component, then plan the points of interaction. Experiment and find out which method works best for you. It really doesn't matter which approach you take just as long as you end up with a fully rounded product.

the sweet KISS of success

For every thousand presentations that go on too long, only one or two will be too short. Very few presentations are literally *too short* (in terms of minutes and seconds), which gives a clue to the next secret of producing good presentations:

KISS

In its polite form this stands for **Keep It Short and Simple.**

- ■ In 20 minutes (including the introduction and the conclusion) you have time for only *two* major points.
- ■ In 30 minutes you might make *three* major points.
- ■ In 40–45 minutes you *might* be able to cover *four* major points, but three points and a longer time for questions would be a better alternative.

Mike Weatherley, one of the producers of the BBC TV programme *Business Matters,* is on record as saying: 'When I'm making a programme, I usually work on the basis that I can get three main points over in the programme.' The fact that a professional TV crew with all the hi-tech equipment and years of expertise at their disposal can't get more than three points across in half an hour is surely a lesson for anyone planning a presentation, no matter how sophisticated their set-up.

something to think about

Most adults have an attention span of somewhere between 25 and 40 minutes, and can only process five to nine chunks of information at any given time. A presentation which contains too many items of information can be too long, even though it lasts for only 15–20 minutes. If you speak for much more than 45 minutes, it really doesn't matter how many points you make – most members of the audience will forget almost everything you say within the first couple of hours after you finish speaking!

You need to have the right amount of content, in a reasonable time span, delivered at an acceptable pace.

it's all in the timing

People come to a presentation to gain information which will be useful to them in some way. They come to *learn*, and they need time to *absorb* the new information. Without that time the information won't get past what is called *short-term memory*, and will soon be lost.

The lower line in this diagram shows how increasing loss of concentration during the middle part of a presentation is directly related to the length of the presentation. Only the

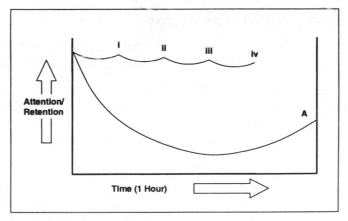

opening (*primary*) and closing (most *recent*) sections are retained to any great extent, and the recovery of attention towards the end of a presentation becomes smaller and smaller, the longer the event goes on.

The upper, wavy line shows the effectiveness of the same material – properly structured – when the presentation is kept to a *maximum* running time of no more than 40 minutes. It really consists of several 'mini-presentations', each with its own lead in and climax. The 'peaks' (i, ii, iii and iv) are built-in *high spots* at 10, 20, 30 and 40 minutes, which actively refocus audience attention, making it easier to maintain concentration *between* the peak points.

on confronting a blank sheet of paper

A blank sheet of paper that must be filled is one of the most daunting objects known to man, so:

Don't start with a blank sheet of paper.

Yes, I'm serious. I've used this process for years, it is highly efficient and can be learnt in a matter of minutes!

the one-man think tank

All you need for this technique is a sheet of plain paper (A4 is OK; A3 size is better), plus a set of coloured pens or pencils.

Lay the paper down with one of the long sides towards you and draw a rectangular box in the centre of the page with a line at each corner. (It is even more effective if you draw the central box and the four lines radiating from it in different colours.)

People who plan their presentations by drawing up a list of the things they plan to say often end up with nothing but a censored series of ideas – in no particular order. If we try to impose some order upon the list, for example by drawing in linking lines, the end result is even more confused.

The list arrangement (above left) is obviously very poor when it comes to showing relationships *between* points. The spidergram (above right), on the other hand, clearly illustrates individual points *and* the overall structure. What can only be *inferred* from the linked list is made patently obvious in the spidergram.

Incidentally, as far as setting out your spidergram is concerned, the following guidelines are recommended:

▪ The 'keyword' in the central box should be a one or two word abbreviation of your primary objective.

- Use just one or two words on each 'limb', even a whole phrase if necessary – but *never* a complete sentence.
- Use the full range of colours you have available.
- If different parts of the spidergram seem to link up, indicate this fact with a linking arrow rather than duplicating a whole set of 'limbs'.

Once you have completed your spidergram you may need to do some serious pruning to bring it back to three main points. It will help to go back to your statement of objectives and start cutting out those parts of your diagram which aren't directly relevant to your primary objective.

all the truth that's fit to present

People tend to respond more readily to upbeat presentations, so concentrate on the *positive* elements of what you want to say and the *negative* aspects of any contrary information. There is nothing wrong in presenting your case in the best possible light so long as you don't use distortions or lies.

Having said that, you must also allow for people's natural cynicism. If you paint too rosy a picture and avoid *all* contrary evidence, your audience is likely to become more than a little suspicious. You can actually strengthen your case by including one or two possible objections – which you then demolish – rather than trying to pretend that no objections exist.

think ahead – plan ahead

Once you think that your basic script is complete, run through it with these three considerations in mind:

- Have you said everything you wanted/needed to say?
- Have you said too much?
- Have you left any obvious hooks for questions?

If necessary, you can now edit your script to resolve any obviously outstanding questions or ambiguous statements, and to remove any 'loose ends'.

You can also script answers to questions that *might* be asked but that you don't want to cover in the presentation.

script, notes or cue cards?

I once asked a particularly impressive speaker how long it had taken to develop such an effortless, flowing style. The gentleman concerned led me on stage and pointed to the top of the lectern, and some 20 cue cards.

'No one can give a good presentation without doing the preparation,' he told me. 'And very few people are skilled enough to work without some kind of notes.

'What you get from experience isn't the ability to skip the ground work – it's the facility to make it *look* like you didn't have to do the ground work!'

So, which *physical* format is most suitable for your text?

Clearly, your presentation style should match your current level of expertise. For example, how good is your memory under pressure? It may look very professional if you appear to be speaking 'off the cuff', but how professional will it look if you say 'Next Monday' when you mean 'A week on Monday', or if you say '27 per cent' when you should have said '72 per cent'?

Some people really can produce a speech at the drop of a hat. Most of us need some form of script.

full script

A full script takes time to prepare since it must be more or less word perfect. If you don't happen to have a professional scriptwriter on hand, you may have to produce several drafts before you get your script worded entirely to your satisfaction.

Using a full script can be a great confidence builder. You cannot forget your lines; there is no danger of leaving something unsaid or of giving incorrect information; and you can time your presentation with considerable accuracy.

On the minus side, it is exceedingly difficult to *write* a script that sounds natural, let alone *read* a script so that it sounds natural. You must constantly break eye contact in order to look down at your script, and you are more or less tied to the lectern or whatever your notes are resting on.

> **tip:**
>
> Modularize your script. Write it so that you can add or remove material in neat chunks if the need arises.

A word-for-word text is also notoriously inflexible. If any part of your script needs to be changed at the last moment you'll just have to cross out the obsolete material and make do with what is left – or learn to write very fast!

notes

It is not unknown for a speaker to use a mind map as the 'notes' for a presentation. It is more common, however, to prepare notes with main headings, sub-headings, and a brief outline of each point that you wish to make. In short, a rough guide to what you want to say.

Using notes means that you have something down in black and white (for confidence building), and in a format that can easily be edited right up to the last moment. If time runs short you can use the same material, but simply deal with each point in less detail.

Notes also allow you to *appear* more spontaneous, since you really will be speaking 'off the cuff', to a certain extent.

The main drawback to using notes is that it is entirely up to you to remember what you meant to say about a particular heading or sub-heading. You will also need a place where you can rest your notes so that you can see them, but the audience can't.

cue cards

Since cue cards (for example, box file cards, approximately 10 centimetres by 15 centimetres) are much smaller than A4 sheets of paper, you will need to work with key *words* and *phrases* rather than sentences.

---

tip:

To avoid getting your cue cards mixed up, number them distinctly in one corner. Or punch a hole in one corner of each card so that they can be held together by a treasury tag or similar fastening.

Using cue cards means that you can carry part of your script with you if you want to move away from the lectern. This will give you virtually unlimited freedom of movement.

The main drawback to using cue cards is the lack of written information. All the cards for a single presentation should fit easily into a jacket pocket or handbag. If they don't, your presentation may be too long, or you're putting too much on your cue cards. Perhaps you would be more comfortable using notes?

visual aids as memory joggers

Using the visual aids as an abbreviated script cuts down on preparation and allows a great deal of flexibility. But you will need to check each visual as you display it, which *could* mean that you spend more time looking at the displays than at the audience. You should also avoid making the visual aids more detailed to compensate for the lack of script or notes.

foil backing sheets

If you have foils with backing sheets, these can be used:

- to carry a copy of the contents of the foil;
- for notes regarding the contents of the foil.

As your presentations skills develop you may find that this is a practical alternative to the options suggested above.

if the cap fits

So the real answer as to how you should prepare your script is really up to you.

Try each of the styles – full script, notes, cue cards or memory joggers – and see which works best for you.

when you come to the end – stop

the intro and the outro

The two parts of your presentation that will be remembered most clearly are the introduction and the conclusion – especially the conclusion. A good ending can sometimes turn a rather mediocre presentation into a success. Likewise, a bad ending can ruin an otherwise excellent presentation, leaving the audience feeling dissatisfied and critical rather than impressed and appreciative.

Always aim to finish a presentation (no matter what the subject) on a positive note. Make the audience feel that you and they have shared in a worthwhile experience. In the old show business adage, 'Always leave them wanting more'.

This will be much easier to achieve if you adhere to the rule that every presentation needs a clear, well-planned *outcome*.

what was it all about?

As we've already seen, the purpose or outcome of a presentation is the foundation stone of the whole structure. The closing section of a presentation is the final and equally vital part of that structure, and must be something more than just the end of the event. It must summarize all that has gone before and create a bridge to whatever happens after the presentation is all over.

What your audience will really need to know is:

- What (are we supposed to do)?
- When (do we do it)?
- How (will we know when we've done it satisfactorily)?

The answers to these questions depend on the intended outcome of the presentation, of course, and your closing remarks should aim to answer the questions as precisely and clearly as possible.

closing comments

One of the most common reasons for lost sales is not that the sales person has made a bad sales pitch, but rather that they didn't *close* the sale. That is to say, having described and demonstrated all the advantages of the product, the salesperson forgot to ask that crucial last question: 'How many would you like?' or 'Will you be paying with cash, a cheque or a credit card?'

Many presentations also fail because the presenter fails to 'close' in an appropriate manner. Three common errors that occur at the end of a presentation are:

the emergency stop

Without a hint of warning the speaker pulls up, in a metaphorical screech of brakes, with a phrase such as:

Well, I think that's all I have to say, so I'll stop there.

The speaker 'thinks' that she has nothing more to say? Didn't she draw up some kind of script? Doesn't she *know* that she has nothing else that needs saying? Maybe she has left something out, but how will the audience ever know?

By the time you come to the end of a presentation, you should have answered the three vital questions What? When? and How? and there should be no need to announce the fact. Nor is it necessary to offer a self-evident observation such as: 'I've finished so I'll stop.'

If you *have* finished, unexpectedly or not, leave it at that and either invite questions or sit down, depending on how the event has been arranged.

the endless maze

The 'endless maze' speaker can be recognized by the way that he ends up as lost and confused as his audience, thus:

> And so I'll finish on that point – and remind you of the comment I made earlier about...

And off he goes again.

It's as though he is lost in some kind of oral maze, frequently sighting the exit but never quite able to reach it before veering off down another detour.

This speaker also isn't working from a well-prepared script or he would have no trouble reaching the exit. Rightly or wrongly, this gives the impression that he simply threw a few major headings together at the last moment, and now he's hoping that if he talks for long enough he is bound to cover all the finer (unscripted) details, sooner or later.

the clichéd climax

Unlike the 'emergency stop', where the speaker seems to arrive at an ending by accident, the 'clichéd climax' presenter obviously knows exactly when she is going to finish – and insists on broadcasting the fact:

In conclusion...
Just before I close...
And finally...
I'd like to leave you with this thought...

It's as if the speaker wants to prepare us for that terrible moment when she will stop speaking and all the joy will go out of our lives.

the more the merrier

All of these examples clearly illustrate the need for a well-ordered structure in any presentation. Not just because it *seems* like a good idea, but because it saves so much trouble in the long run – as in the case of the style of ending I've dubbed 'the more the merrier':

Favourite phrases this time include:

And in addition...
I'd also like to say/point out/remind you...

Unlike the 'endless maze', where the speaker keeps harking back to earlier comments, when a 'more the merrier' speaker reaches the end of a presentation it is not an ending after all, but a new beginning. The process of summing up his ideas seems to generate a whole series of new thoughts. The audience, on the other hand, can only remain attentive for a limited amount of time.

Last-minute ideas, no matter how brilliant, should be saved for another day unless they genuinely dovetail into the points set out in your script – and are *essential* to the effectiveness of the presentation.

know when to stop

Speakers often fall into 'endless maze' or 'more the merrier' mode when they find that they have finished ahead of time – and thereby snatch defeat from the very jaws of success.

To put it bluntly, few presentations fail by ending early – unless the premature ending is due to lack of adequate preparation. If you can say everything you want and/or need to say in less than your allotted time that is a bonus, not an error. Don't spoil the effect by trying to pad your speech up to the 'official' length. Make the most of the situation by allowing an extended question and answer session or by inserting an extra comfort break.

happy endings

Having described some 'presentation pitfalls', let's move on now to get some ideas on how it *should* be done.

the closing summary

A closing summary, though useful in almost any setting, is most suitable when the presentation itself is only intended to communicate information and doesn't require any follow-up activity by the members of the audience. Carefully avoiding clichés such as:

So, before I finish I'd just like to summarize the points we've covered this afternoon...

You can proceed straight into the summary with no introduction at all, as in:

> So, we've seen what kind of pressures the company faces (*list the pressures*), and the possible ways in which those pressures can be handled (*list the alternatives*)...

the challenge

Issuing a challenge to the audience is used to best effect where a particular problem has been addressed, or where you are calling for greater or renewed effort.

Couch the challenge in terms of what 'we can' do, or 'we will' do, and state a precise course of action in this context. A mere emotional appeal for some (unspecified) action may be very rousing at the time, but it is likely to lead to confusion and/or apathy when the members of the audience actually try to put your rhetoric into practice.

the 'call to action'

When the main intention is to generate agreement on a particular course of action, you may find it more effective to use persuasion rather than a challenge. To this end it is valid to confine your summation to the points *in favour* of the proposed action and to end by stating precisely what the next step should be.

Since you will presumably have covered any contradictory arguments – and answered them – in the course of your presentation, it is unnecessary to state them all over again. One of the most outstanding examples of a *call to action* ending was used at the climax of a political rally, when the party leader exhorted his followers to: 'Go home and prepare to rule!'

As it turned out, the call was somewhat over optimistic. No matter. Its purpose was to grab newspaper headlines and create a positive attitude in the conference hall. In both respects it was hugely successful.

the 'feel good' factor

Motivational speakers aim to leave the audience with a warm glow rather than indicating some further course of action. This would work well in the closing session of a multi-presentation event where you wish to reinforce the group identity, for example, but is out of place at a relatively impersonal event such as a press conference.

The two most popular forms of the 'feel good' ending make use of a quotation or a piece of poetry respectively. In both cases the material should be short and to the point, though the 'point' in question does not have to be directly linked to the subject of the presentation. As long as the material is highly emotionally charged, the precise nature of the quotation or poem will be dictated by the emotional response you wish to arouse in your audience, rather than by the subject of the presentation.

beware the red light

If you've ever watched a political conference on TV you've probably noticed the coloured lights that are used to signal to speakers when their time is up. You may also have noticed how often speakers start to panic when the warning light comes on, despite the fact that they must surely have known how much time they would have when they were preparing their speech.

There are times, of course, when jokes get more laughs and bold declarations get more applause than the speaker expected, which has thrown their timing out. This is why a well-prepared speaker always arms himself with two copies of his closing comments.

One copy is based on the assumption that nothing unforeseen will happen, and the speaker will have all the time that he needs to wrap up the presentation at his own speed. The second copy, (the copy that so many speakers overlook) is set out on the basis that everything that *can* go wrong *will* go wrong and that he will need to wind up his comments in very short order indeed.

The length of the 'emergency' ending will depend on the length of the presentation as a whole. If your entire speech lasts only five or ten minutes then allow one or two minutes for your *long* ending, and 30–45 seconds for the emergency ending (that's about 60–90 words at the average speaking pace). If your presentation is scheduled for 30–40 minutes (or more!) then the two endings would be longer – but not too much longer.

curtain up!

the 'magic minute'

Within 5–10 *seconds* of your entrance every member of your audience will have formed a subconscious opinion of you. In the next 50–55 seconds that opinion will be confirmed, or perhaps qualified, but almost never undone!

The members of an audience react to everything they see and hear, and the overall impact of a presentation will be enhanced by anything up to 18 or 20 per cent by a well-judged introduction. It must first act as a 'hook' to catch your audience's attention, and then go on to:

- command attention;
- create a framework;
- set the mood;
- create motivation;
- establish credibility;
- summarize your message;
- indicate whether batteries are included;
- set out your time lines.

Let's start, then, by looking at some of the different ways in which you can 'hook' the audience's attention.

quotations

There are a number of excellent books of quotations on the market, but be sure to select a quote that is appropriate, and from someone who will have credibility with your audience:

'As Winston Churchill once said...'
'As Mabel Ramsbotham once observed...'

Most people have at least a vague idea that Winston Churchill was someone famous and important. But who cares what Mabel Ramsbotham once observed? Unless, of course, she is a well-respected colleague, a department head or the managing director, in which case her opinion may well count for a lot more than the thoughts of Winston Churchill.

humour

There are two basic forms of humour – *instinctive* and *deliberate*. Instinctive humour grows out of the presentation material – the sort of humour 'you had to be there to appreciate'.

Deliberate humour, on the other hand, encompasses jokes, funny stories, cartoons and so on. If you're seriously considering using 'deliberate' humour in your presentation, I suggest that you think long and hard – and then change your mind. One genuinely funny, *relevant* story will work far better than half a dozen jokes.

The important questions to ask yourself about *any* kind of humour are:

■ Will people understand it (as you intended it)?
■ Will they find it funny?

If you're not sure on either count, try something else.

questions

Asking a question right at the start of a presentation is a good way of letting your audience know that you wish to communicate *with* them, rather than simply lecture *at* them.

For the best effect ask the audience a question that only allows for an unqualified 'Yes/No' answer (preferably 'Yes'), such as 'Can you hear me at the back?'

Also make sure that you are asking for a manageable response. The question: 'Is the seating comfortable?' is certainly relevant. But what do you do if a majority of the audience answer 'No'?

visual impact

You could wait until everyone is seated, then leap on to the stage wearing a gorilla suit and waving a bunch of bananas. Or then again, maybe not.

Whilst fashions in general are becoming more relaxed, many people still believe that 'clothes make the man – or woman', and they will happily judge you on your physical appearance – and nothing else. If you want people to take notice of what you have to say, dress as far as possible to meet your audience's expectations.

The classic 'power outfit' for men is a dark suit, white shirt, a conservatively patterned tie with plenty of crimson or scarlet (not pillar box red!). Socks should be plain navy blue or black. Shoes should be black, in good repair and well polished. (Judging a man by the state of his shoes is far more common in business circles than you might imagine.)

For women, changing attitudes mean that it is no longer necessary to wear a female version of the male power outfit described above. 'Classic' outfits, such as a blazer or collarless jacket with a skirt, trouser suits and dresses, are all acceptable. Colour schemes should be sober (though not sombre), and chosen to complement individual hair, eye and skin coloration.

Items to avoid include lacy tops, floppy collars, conspicuous jewellery and scarves which need constant adjustment.

By the way, if the presentation is anything but a formal business event, is there any chance that people might be in doubt about what kind of clothes *they* should wear (formal business suit, smart casual or whatever)? It can save a lot of embarrassment if you specify the correct dress mode in the invitation to the presentation.

topical references

Topical references can be used to great effect, as long as they are genuinely relevant to the subject under discussion – and everyone knows what you're talking about.

personal anecdotes

These must be *very* appropriate, and brief, to justify their use. I still remember an event from quite some time ago, where the speaker opened his presentation with a personal anecdote that started: 'You know, I nearly didn't live long enough to make this presentation...'

At that moment he had the unqualified attention of everyone in the room. By the time he struggled to the end of the story, some three or four minutes later, most people in the audience were thinking, 'So what?'

shocking statistics

If you want to use a shocking statistic – to get your audience's attention without actually insulting them – then make it as simple but as hard-hitting as possible. Something like:

> Seventy-five per cent of all retired people are living on a greatly reduced income. Thirty per cent of all retired people are living on or below the poverty line. The material we're going to cover in this presentation could save you becoming a part of those statistics!

Used well, shocking statistics can be extremely effective, as long as you remember that statistics are easily misunderstood, unless the information is kept short and simple.

outrageous statements

> Speaker (*to audience of computer programmers*): 'Do you realize that you are wasting your time if you don't have a competent technical author to prepare your documentation!'
> *[Short pause]*
> 'At least, that's how your customers may see it.'

From the audience's point of view this was definitely a highly contentious opening, but it achieved its purpose.

The 'outrageous statement' opening will undoubtedly make your audience sit up and take notice, and if it (gently) ruffles a few feathers it may also help the audience to remember the message when a more gentlemanly, neutral presentation has long since faded from memory.

teasers

One trainer I used to work with liked to have the following four instructions written up on a flip chart or white board *before* the delegates started to arrive:

- ■ Make mistakes.
- ■ Ask 'dumb' questions.
- ■ Cheat.
- ■ Have fun.

Once the delegates were assembled he would explain that the four points meant:

- ■ Nobody is perfect, so understand that making mistakes is a valuable element in the learning process.

- ■ If you don't understand something, say so, it's part of my job to make this as clear as I can.
- ■ Forget everything you learnt in school about not looking at other people's work. In business we work best when we pool our knowledge and our expertise.
- ■ Treat this course as an *opportunity*, not as an obligation. The more you enjoy the course, the more effectively will you absorb the course material.

maps and shoehorns

Once your audience is satisfactorily 'hooked' there are other functions an introduction must serve.

In one situation you may want to calm and reassure your audience, whilst on another occasion it may be an essential part of the presentation that you get them stirred up and excited. In either case, one way of achieving the required result might be to 'draw a map' of the 'territory' you intend to cover in your presentation.

This is also an effective way of dealing with a situation where you know that different members of the audience have quite different views on the main topic of the presentation. In this case, the purpose of the 'mapping' process is to provide a clear, definitive view of the topic. You can't expect everyone to fall in line with your definition automatically, of course, but at least it will be plain to all concerned just where the presentation is coming from – and where you plan to go.

Just how detailed your map needs to be will depend on whether your audience has any (relevant) prior knowledge of the topic being discussed. In some situations, the people in your audience may have nearly as much information as you have yourself, in which case it is simply a question of fleshing out that knowledge so that they can make a decision, undertake a particular course of action, or whatever.

If you find that your audience knows little or nothing about the subject of the presentation then your initial map must be more detailed than normal. But not so detailed that it becomes a summary of everything that you are going to talk about.

Think of it rather as a shoehorn, helping to ease the audience into the subject. Introduce some small part of your topic by relating it to something that the members of the audience will already know about and which matters to them. This will reassure them that your topic is comprehensible, and that the presentation is relevant to their current situation/future needs. It will also give them the confidence to follow along, even if things get a little complicated and technical later on.

setting a mood

How do you want your audience to feel as the presentation starts? Relaxed? Alert? Critical? Receptive?

Your opening remarks will play a crucial role in setting the mood of the whole presentation. Would you open a presentation with a shocking statistic or statement if you wanted the audience to feel relaxed and receptive? Would you try to stir your sales force to greater efforts by the use of soft lights and a 'fireside chat'?

For maximum effect you must analyse your audience as far as possible, and then make a best guess as to what kind of approach will produce the required response from that particular set of people. Above all, *never* assume that any two audiences will react the same way to the same material; they won't.

creating motivation

The best way to motivate your audience can be summed up in the question, 'What's in it for me?'

This may seem rather mercenary but, as Dale Carnegie points out in *How to Win Friends and Influence People*, self-interest is an incredibly effective source of motivation.

To make people take notice of what you have to say, you must give them a reason to listen, a reason which relates to their own experience.

Talk to your audience as they are, not as you would like them to be. This, too, will benefit from as much audience analysis as you can manage. Some members of your audience may have been 'volunteered', rather than choosing to come of their own accord. Don't let this put you off. It may actually be easier to sell the presentation to those people if you can only show them that they aren't going to be wasting their time after all.

American psychologist Abraham Maslow has described what might be called a *hierarchy of motivation*:

The pyramid represents various levels of achievement. Maslow argued that people can only be motivated to move up to the next level when they have satisfactorily met the basic requirements of their current level. You are unlikely to have much success encouraging a company to embark on a major reorganization when their most pressing need is to find enough money to pay their suppliers!

For maximum effect, then, you must *engage* your audience's attention at their *current* level, and then show them how your presentation will fulfil their natural inclination to move up to the next level of motivation.

establishing credibility

Establishing your credentials is a surprisingly delicate affair. A string of academic and/or professional qualifications and details of your years as the right hand of God may sound impressive, but you are far more likely to achieve rapport if you adopt a style of introduction that is more gentle on your audience's self-respect.

are batteries included?

Always let your audience know whether some kind of follow-up action will be expected of them, and how they can tell when they have successfully completed the required task. The phrase 'Sales must rise' may sound like a clear objective at the time, yet it really doesn't say very much at all. Which sales must rise? How much must they rise by? Over what period of time?

making and breaking expectations

It is always a good move to show your audience that you are aware of their expectations, and to clear up any misconceptions that you know or believe exist regarding the reason(s) for the presentation. Get your audience to believe that you are all there for a common purpose and see how it builds rapport.

providing a framework

People find it easier to absorb new information if they can relate it to the knowledge that they already possess – hence the repetitive nature of the guideline:

Tell them what you're going to tell them.
Tell them.
Tell them what you've told them – and why.

Wherever it is appropriate, always aim to use your introduction to create a bridge from the audience's existing knowledge to your *new* information.

times and events

When several presentations follow on from one another, set people's minds at rest (and thereby make them more receptive) by explaining the total situation, not just your part of it.

Some presenters talk through a foil listing events and times. Alternatively, you might include a timetable as part of the initial handout and then use a foil to *confirm* that everything will go as planned, or to explain any alterations to the programme.

Incidentally, when you say your presentation will last for 10, or 20 or 30 minutes, make sure it doesn't run for 15, 25 or 35 minutes.

never say not!

Human beings cannot think in negatives. If I say to you: 'Don't think of a pig in a straw hat riding a bicycle', it's extremely likely that the very first thing you will do is think of a pig in a straw hat riding a bicycle – and quite naturally so. After all, how can you be sure that you aren't thinking about something, unless you first have a clear idea what it is that you're not going to think about?

By the same logic, if I say 'I'm *not* here to sell you anything', your subconscious mind hears: 'I'm here to sell you anything – not.' Which means that by the time you get to 'not' you've already heard me say that I *am* here to sell you something!

So, if there's something you don't want the audience to think about – *leave it out*. If you say it, they'll think about it, no matter *how* carefully you phrase it.

selecting and using visual aids

just for effect?

Why use visual aids? Just consider the following facts:

- We learn about 90% of what we know *visually* – from films, books, etc. Only 7–11% is learnt through hearing alone.
- The average audience member will remember about 70% of a purely verbal presentation three hours later, and as little as 10% only three days later.
- Of a purely visual presentation, about 75% will be remembered after three hours, and up to 20% after three days.
- About 85% of a mixed verbal/visual presentation will be recalled after three hours, and as much as 66% will be remembered after three days.
- Presenters who use visual aids are generally perceived as being more professional and persuasive than those who rely on speech alone.

In short, for a truly powerful and *memorable* presentation you will need to include some form of visual aid.

horses for courses

Having examined the advantages, it is only fair to point out that visual aids can only be justified when used well. From the options available to you, think very carefully about which form of visual aid will best suit your purpose, your audience and your own skill.

(It is advisable to avoid using different kinds of visual aid simultaneously unless you have professional assistance – and plenty of practice.)

chalkboard

'Chalk and Talk' is rapidly becoming a synonym for the most ineffective, hidebound form of training. While this medium is certainly cheap, it is also extremely limited and really only suitable for small groups (a dozen or less), and where more modern facilities are not available.

whiteboard and pen

Although a whiteboard shows colours far more effectively than a chalkboard, you will still need to have presentable handwriting to make the best use of this medium. If in doubt, always use block capital letters, not 'joined up' lettering. Whiteboards are suitable for informal meetings, such as discussion groups and brainstorming, and for ad hoc displays in formal meetings (as an alternative to a flipchart). Audience size (maximum 20–30) will depend on the quality of your handwriting.

> **tip:**
>
> Some whiteboard/flipchart pens use spirit-based ink which evaporates very easily when exposed to the air, so always put the cap back on a pen as soon as you stop writing.

One of the main drawbacks to using a whiteboard is the lack of any permanent record of what was written/drawn on the board once it has been cleaned off, though electronic whiteboards are now available which will give an A4-sized printout of the current contents of the writing area.

flipcharts

Flipcharts can be a mixed blessing. They are relatively cheap – but can be hard to handle. They are suitable for multi-coloured displays, but some types of ink tend to 'bleed' through flipchart-type paper. Once again, the presenter's handwriting skills will affect the advisability of using this medium. If you usually have to decipher your writing for other readers, avoid flipcharts.

Flipcharts can be used to great effect with groups of up to 30 people, especially when it is necessary to record lists of ideas or display 'spur of the moment' information.

Individual pages and sequences can be prepared in advance and/or built up as the presentation goes along, and pages can be torn off and stuck up on the wall with Blu-tack to create an expanding display.

---

tips:

1. To find pages easily in a set of pre-prepared flipchart pages, make a sellotape tag for each page down the side of the chart where you usually stand.
2. If you know that you will have to draw a quite complicated chart or diagram during the presentation, lightly pencil it in beforehand, then simply follow the pencil lines.

---

overhead projector (OHP)

The OHP has become one of the most widely used visual aids in business presentations. Given an adequate screen and appropriate seating arrangements it is suitable for almost any size of audience up to the low hundreds.

To get the best image with an OHP, the screen should, ideally, be at right angles to a line drawn from the centre of the screen to the centre of the projection mirror (see illustration). Thus a wall, even a plain white one, is *not* an entirely satisfactory alternative to a proper screen.

As a general rule, the size of screen for a given venue can be calculated using the ratio of 1:6; thus, if the last row of seats is 14 metres from the screen, the screen should be 14/6 = 2.3 metres square. (Minimum screen size should be about 1.5 metres square.)

Foils are a very flexible medium and are suitable for formal or informal presentations, especially where any type of graphical information is involved.

The main advantages of an OHP are its ease of use and the option of switching between various display styles. Foils may be used:

- In straight display mode where the entire foil is immediately visible.
- As a sequence of overlays, to build up a complex picture.
- In 'progressive revelation' fashion, whereby points are revealed one at a time by sliding a mask down the foil.

The main disadvantage of using an OHP is the difficulty of ensuring that everyone can see the whole screen, especially those people sitting in the first few rows:

This situation is almost inevitable unless the OHP is correctly positioned on a purpose-built stand. It is the main reason why you should never use the whole area of an OHP foil.

■ Text on an OHP foil should be *at least* 6–7 mm in height (that's between 24 pt and 28 pt), and will need to increase to about 15 mm (or 60 pt) if any part of the audience will be more than 13–15 m away from the screen. (4 pts = 1 mm approx.)

■ Always use foils in the 'landscape' position to minimize poor visibility, and leave a margin of about 2.5 cm on all four sides of the foil. Do not use the bottom third of the foil at all if you can possibly avoid it.

■ Ten to twelve words on each foil is a sensible maximum. If a foil is too 'busy', your audience will happily ignore what you are saying until they have read the foil all the way through – or until you move on to the next foil.

In the example above, the foil on the left actually contains four separate headings. The foil on the right shows the first heading set out correctly (the rest of the left-hand foil should have been divided to make three further foils, following the same basic guidelines).

slides

Slide projection is a medium suitable for audiences of almost any size up to 1,000 or more, but again depends on screen size and the power of the projector.

The slides themselves can be relatively expensive to produce, though well-produced slides, properly used, will undoubtedly bring an air of professionalism to any presentation. Computer graphics packages have the ability to produce high-quality visuals which can be transferred to slides. For larger audiences this medium is undoubtedly one of the best ways of presenting all types of information.

---

tips:

There are still some presenters who insist on turning a projector off and on again each time they change foils or slides, or when they do not have a display for the topic they are currently discussing. This is a throwback to the days when the room was usually blacked out in order to ensure that the projected image was clear to the whole audience.

Today, when the projectors are far more powerful and the presentation room is, at most, in semi-darkness, this is actually bad practise. Each time you turn the projector on and off, you increase the chance of bulb failure.

Leave the projector running when you change foils, and use a neutral foil (the company logo or a plain black or navy blue panel, for example) when you don't have a display for a particular section of the presentation.

Incidentally, although projected displays often work best when the room is in semi-darkness, remember that these conditions are also ideal for falling asleep, especially after lunch! It is better to design clearly visible visual aids, which make good use of colour, with strong contrasts where appropriate, than to rely entirely on the power of the projector.

computer-based displays

There are, in fact, not one but three ways of utilizing computer-generated displays in a presentation context:

1. Connecting a computer to one or more large-screen TVs is simple, practical and very cost effective.
2. A video projection package – either fixed or portable.
3. An LCD Projection Panel, coupled with an OHP, will allow you to project an enlarged version of an ordinary computer screen.

When I first wrote about the video projector option, some five years ago, the most common options were either a presentation room with a permanently mounted projector, or a hire package. (Hire packages typically consisted of a large screen (about 1.2 metres square) with surround, a large three colour video projector, and a computer, plus remote control, connecting cables, etc.) This meant that video projection equipment was really only suitable for larger, properly stage-managed, pre-planned events.

Today there are an ever-increasing number of extremely portable projectors which will accept multiple simultaneous connections, to computer, VC player, etc. Although the top of the range models are still quite costly, prices continue to fall, and this is now a serious option for any company that regularly runs presentations which can benefit from this kind of flexibility.

In a well-equipped setting, including multiple screens, it should be quite possible to cater for audiences of a hundred or more delegates. The ideal situation for using a computer-based display is one where it is necessary that the audience see a computer application up and running. This would typically be where a new piece of software is being demonstrated for sales or training purposes.

Alternatively, using a product such as Microsoft's *PowerPoint*, you can create a dynamic presentation which runs itself and can be tailored to the needs of a specific audience.

The falling price and increasing portability of video projectors has had a correspondingly negative effect on the use of LCD panels. Not least, I suspect, because it was often difficult to display a computer's complete screen area on an LCD panel. This, together with the fact that many video projectors are just as portable, and usually more rugged than the LCD alternative, has cancelled out whatever advantages once made the LCD panels such an attractive option.

The computer/TV set up, the video projector and the LCD projection panels can all be used in almost any setting, and virtually at a moment's notice.

---

tip:

Always run a complete pre-presentation check, including the remote control. If you are using an LCD panel, make sure that the light in the OHP is bright enough to give a clear image.

The biggest drawback to using any kind of *projected* computer output of any kind is the expense. Both options will cost hundreds of pounds per day to hire, or several thousand pounds to purchase outright.

video

Videotape technology, when used well, can add an invaluable air of professionalism to what would otherwise be no more than an adequate presentation. It can be used for both formal and informal meetings, product presentations, training sessions, etc. But it is *not* usually appropriate where the information involves detailed graphics, statistical information, etc.

It is also unsuitable when communicating sensitive information within a company – changes in working practices, mergers, downsizing, etc. Paradoxically, according to an Institute of Management study carried out in the early 1990s, though 60 per cent of large British companies were using videos to communicate important changes, 75 per cent recognized that this was actually an ineffective medium for that particular kind of communication. Other studies have shown a consistently low acceptance of video amongst employees, with UK employees rating it thirteenth out of sixteen alternative means of communication, and US employees rating it eleventh out of fourteen.

Without special equipment a video presentation is limited to an audience of no more than 20–30, but this figure jumps to several hundred when using a high-powered video projector or multiple screens.

tip:

No matter how reliable the source from which you obtain a video, even if it comes from the company learning centre, always run a videotape *right through* the night before you intend to use it. Nothing is worse than to find that a tape is in first class condition except for a loss of picture and/or sound right in the middle of an important statement or explanation.

If you ever try shooting your own video presentation, you will quickly discover why a professionally produced video costs so much to make. Pre-recorded videos, on the other hand, can be hired or purchased from a number of companies at reasonable cost. The video presentation is particularly appropriate, and cost effective, when you want to get the same information or message to several groups at a number of separate events.

film

Film, though still in use as a presentation medium, is becoming very much the exception rather than the rule. Most of the information that once came on film – training materials, health and safety presentations, company PR material, etc – is now available on video instead. And why not? Videotape is both easier to use and much cheaper than film.

Having said that, film has the advantage that it can be used just as easily in small groups as it can for an audience of thousands (depending on use of appropriate equipment and screen size). Despite the relatively high production costs, a well-made film carries a high 'impressiveness' rating, which makes it particularly suitable for large, formal presentations, such as AGMs, product launches, etc.

---

tip:

Film can be quite delicate, especially hire films that have seen extensive use. If it is at all possible, always have an experienced projectionist on hand (even for small, in-house presentations).

The great weakness of film is its inflexibility. Once a film is ready for showing it cannot easily be changed without incurring considerable expense. Creating back-up copies is impossible without the use of expensive professional facilities.

designing effective visual aids

planning screen and flipchart displays

A foil or slide is most productive if it is a focus of attention. A display with three or four bullet points, with three to five words per point, will be far more efficient than a screen full of text.

The following exercise is designed to help you to make your foils as simple yet as powerful as possible:

1. Produce a foil that includes *all* the points and details that you think should be on it.
2. Project the foil and time yourself to see how long it takes to read *everything* on it.
3. If it takes much more than six seconds to read a particular foil or slide, then it needs editing!
4. Check to see how much of the text (if any) is simply a direct copy of part of your spoken material.

5. Cross out everything that isn't *absolutely necessary*. If you still have anything larger than key words/phrases, you haven't finished editing.
6. If more than four to five bullet points are left, either merge some of the points, or split them up over several foils.
7. If a rehearsal leaves you changing foils almost as fast as you can speak, your bullet points are too detailed. Replan your foils so that the bullet points are less specific.

points that make a point

Why do so many presenters depend on a series of anonymous black 'bullet points'? In a book like this black 'bullets' are fine, but in a situation where each display stays up for a minute or more it is worth replacing the standard 'black blob' with something more creative:

UK Sales 2000	Going for it The Three Ps
☺ **1st Qtr 10%**	☞ **Perseverance**
☹ **2nd Qtr (2.1%)**	☞ **Penetration**
☺ **3rd Qtr 12.3%**	☞ **Profits**
☺ **4th Qtr 15.8%**	

These two foils are actually pure text, and text can be used just like graphics. In the next example it is the *visual* impact which makes the display so effective (the top line reads: 'Verbal Content = 7 per cent'):

Verbal Content = 7 per cent

Vocal Interest = 38 per cent

Body Language = 55 per cent

We could present the same information in more scientific manner using a pie chart:

O₁ we can make it more eye-catching by using a touch of humour:

a chart (or graph) for all reasons

Charts and graphs can be an invaluable way of presenting numerical data in an easily understood format. But what is the *best* way of illustrating a particular piece of information?

- ■ **KISS** (Keep It Short and Simple). If the audience does not get the message in five to ten seconds, they'll be watching the screen when they should be listening to you.
- ■ Careful use of colours makes the information more interesting and more memorable.
- ■ Use four lines per graph at most, and use a different colour for each line if the graph shows more than one line.

- ■ *Line graphs* are best suited to illustrate trends over a period of time, such as 'rolling' sales figures and so on. They are not suitable for illustrating precise values.
- ■ Avoid *vertical* labels in a line graph. They are hard to read and therefore easily misread.

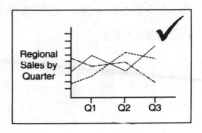

■ To minimize the differences in a chart or graph make the X *axis* (the base line) as long as possible (within reason).

■ To maximize the differences in a chart or graph make the vertical Y *axis* as long as possible.

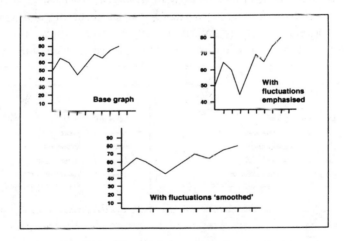

■ In any kind of *bar chart*, limit each display to six or seven bars (or groups of bars) at the most.

■ Use a vertical *bar chart* (with bars running from top to bottom) to compare related data at several points in time.

- It is sometimes quite difficult to compare the information in different bars in a *'stacked' bar chart*.
- So only use 'stacked' columns if the precise make-up of each column is relatively unimportant, otherwise groups of adjacent bars are more effective.
- A *horizontal bar chart* (histogram) is best suited to showing relative values for a number of related items at a given moment in time, and where the main purpose of the chart is to illustrate relative values.

 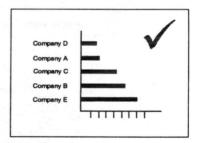

- When using a histogram *always* arrange the bars in ascending or descending order of magnitude, *not* in alphabetical order.
- A *pie chart* is often the best way of illustrating the relative values which go together to make up a single whole (for example, how a given market is currently shared out between the various manufacturers).

- Always put the labels for a pie chart *outside* the chart.
- Keep *pie charts* down to a maximum of six or seven wedges. If necessary, group some of the less important or very closely connected items under a single heading.
- Use a 'floating wedge' when you want to focus attention on that particular section of the pie (and never use more than one floating wedge per chart).

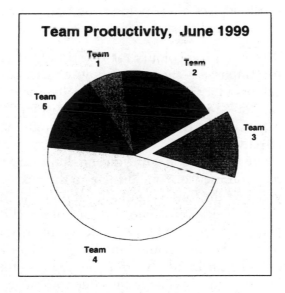

using colour

The last 10–20 years have seen a growing interest in the activities of the two sides of the human brain. Without going into too much detail, it is fair to say that a presentation will have a far greater effect if it is aimed at *both* sides of the brain rather than just the *left* side, as is the case in the traditional, word-oriented style of public speaking.

One way of capturing the right-brain's attention is to use visual aids – which is why this book has two whole chapters on their design, selection and use rather than the standard two or three pages. It is also worth noting that visual aids which make use of *colour* are generally more effective than black-and-white foils, slides, etc. Indeed, a study by the publishing company McGraw-Hill has shown that simply adding colour to an OHP foil (without making *any* other design changes) can improve audience retention of the data on that foil by almost 20 per cent.

The list below gives a few pointers on how your audience is likely to perceive and react to your use of colour:

- When you use colours for text and in diagrams, aim for emphasis – not a rainbow effect. Two or three colours in a single display is usually fine; four colours can look rather excessive; and a display with five or more colours is likely to be more mind-boggling than effective.
- There is no reason why you shouldn't vary the colours that you use from one display to the next – as long as you bear the following qualification in mind.

  If you develop some sort of colour code through your first few foils (say black for main text, red for primary keywords and blue for secondary keywords), don't be surprised if your audience looks totally blank if you suddenly change the code to orange, green and purple for no obvious reason.

■ Always remember that *red* and *green* are the two colours most frequently involved in cases of colour blindness (which affects approximately 10 per cent of men and 0.5 per cent of women). It is a good idea to avoid these two colours when you want to emphasize a difference or a comparison.

---

tip:

When planning to use a variety of different colours – on a foil, slide or flipchart – you can test their comparative *tones* (which even a person suffering from colour blindness can see) by setting out the colours on a piece of white paper and then making a black-and-white photocopy. If you cannot see a difference between any two 'colours' on the photocopied version, then there is a good chance that a colour-blind person may not detect any difference either.

■ The colour *red* should be used, in moderation, for items which you wish to *emphasize*. It is an active, exciting colour (in its lighter, brighter shades) and will help to make the text/diagram more memorable.

■ A bright, warm *yellow* is a good colour for attracting attention (when used on the right background – royal blue, dark green, maroon or sandy brown, for example). It is generally associated with positive things – sunshine, summer, warmth, etc. Unfortunately, it is also virtually invisible when used on a plain white background.

■ *Dark blue* is often associated with a desire for relaxation and a degree of personal privacy. This interpretation may help to explain why medium to dark blue is best used for items which are relatively unimportant (or which you *don't* want to draw attention to).

- *Light blue*, like yellow, has positive connotations linked to clear skies, sunny days and so on. (It's no accident that *faded* denim jeans are much more popular than brand new, *dark* blue garments.) Unfortunately, *light blue* and similar colours – pale turquoise, for instance – are visually weak unless set off by complementary colours nearby.
- Although there are certain difficulties involved in using *green* and *red* together, *green* itself, in its darker shades, is a visually strong colour and is the most visible colour under poor lighting conditions.

---

tip:

When selecting colours in a computer graphics program, it is useful to know what is meant by 'Hue', 'Sat' and 'Lum'.

Hue simply means 'colour'. Changing the Hue setting will give different colours (red, yellow, green, etc) of equal brightness and intensity.

Sat is short for 'saturation', or the intensity of the colour. Maximum saturation gives the most intense version of a colour; minimum saturation produces a shade of grey.

Lum is an abbreviation of luminescence, or brightness (the presence or absence of light). For any colour, the maximum luminescence will produce white, while the minimum setting will produce black.

- Generally speaking, it is a good idea to avoid the lighter shades of *green* (that is, the shades which have a large element of *yellow* in them, such as *lime-green*). These colours have very negative associations in many peoples' minds, related to sickness, etc.
- Incidentally, medium to light shades of *green* show up very badly on a white background or under a bright light.

last word on graphics

Always check whether your graphics, especially your intended colour scheme, will work in real life. All too often, inexperienced presenters assume that the effect they see on their computer will be duplicated in the presentation room. And all too often they are wrong.

Some key points to watch out for are:

- A colour that looks good in small doses doesn't necessarily look as good when used as a main background colour. Often the exact reverse is true.
- Print that can be read clearly on the computer screen may not be anything like as clear to the people sitting in the back row at the presentation. In practice, as we said in the last chapter, anything smaller than 28 pt is likely to be unreadable from more than a metre away, and in many cases even larger fonts may be appropriate.
- Colour contrasts that are plainly readable on the computer screen may be totally illegible in the presentation room. Here, again, the exact opposite is often true. A frequent error is the use of white lettering on a medium to light background colour. In practice, white lettering, especially small white lettering, is only practical on a dark background such as navy blue or black.

handouts

A handout, be it text, graphics or both, provides a *visual* reinforcement for the other elements of a presentation.

Apart from anything else, there is always the problem of ensuring that the members of the audience interpret your message accurately. Those with an *auditory* PTS (Primary

Thinking Style) may be completely comfortable with a purely verbal presentation. But they only make up about 25 per cent of the business population. The other 75 per cent need that back-up material or there are likely to be significant gaps in their version of what you said – which will be filled in with what they think you probably said.

Those members of the audience who have a high level of *right-brain* activity may find it relatively difficult to stay attentive if your presentation follows the usual progression from individual facts up to overall picture. An interesting and imaginative handout will help to focus their attention.

In short, a handout helps to ensure that your audience gets the message, the whole message and nothing but the message.

But when should you hand out the handouts: before, during or after the presentation?

- If you distribute the handout(s) *before* the presentation (by leaving a copy on each seat, or by handing them to people as they come in) you really have no control over what people do with the handout.
- If you distribute handouts at the start of each *subsection* of an event, some people may read ahead but at least they will be limited to material that is to be covered within the current session.
- If you don't make the handout(s) available until *after* the event (by having someone pass them out as people leave, perhaps) you can be sure that no one will read ahead.

On the other hand:

- People don't usually get diverted by the handout(s) unless they are bored with the presentation.
- If the presentation is mainly a detailed explanation of the foils in the handout, people will appreciate being able to make notes directly alongside the relevant illustrations.

■ It is a presenter's job to produce an interesting and informative presentation – not to police the audience.

The key factor that decides when to circulate a handout is purely utilitarian: when should it be distributed to achieve the greatest benefit for the maximum number of people?

colour in handouts

If you ever think of producing handouts on coloured paper, you may be interested to know that the most readable colour combination is *black* print on a *canary yellow* background. Such a document would be even more stimulating (with negligible loss of visibility) if an occasional pastel pink/blue/green page were included amongst the yellow.

Generally speaking, it is more effective to use coloured pages sparingly in a handout.

and then the lights went out

What would you do if your entire presentation revolves around some kind of electrical equipment and at the very last moment it all breaks down?

Worse still, what are you going to do if something goes wrong with the equipment during your presentation?

■ You can panic.
■ You can fall back on *Plan B*.

Any presenter who works with electrical devices should always have a Plan B. With a good Plan B, you can carry on regardless (using a different medium), instead of grinding to a humiliating halt as you hear that delicate 'pop' of exploding equipment.

Your personal Plan B will depend on which visual aids you are using, but here is one of the most common back-up systems.

No matter whether you're using an OHP or slide projector, a video or a film, be sure to duplicate all your main displays on a flipchart (flipcharts never blow a fuse or a bulb).

This means extra work, of course, but if you ever have to fall back on Plan B it will save your presentation and your face.

And if nothing goes wrong? Then at least you will have had the comfort and reassurance of knowing that you were prepared for any eventuality.

setting the scene

anyone for tennis?

When it comes to setting up your display facilities – flipchart, OHP or slide projector, etc – there are two basic options. The first alternative – the 'head on' position – places the screen directly facing the audience. The second option requires that the screen be placed to one side and at an angle to the audience.

If the screen is placed at an angle to the audience they must look at you, or the screen, but not both. If the screen is placed centre stage they can see the display and you at the same time.

Assuming that you have designed your foils or slides correctly, they should be simple enough to focus the viewers' attention on what you are saying, thereby reinforcing it.

Incidentally, you may not have a choice about where the screen is positioned. Many presentation facilities have the screen in a fixed location (usually in the 'head on' position). If you are likely to be doing a number of presentations, working at several different sites, it is worth practising with both set-ups so that you feel comfortable in either setting.

please be seated

Once you have located your screen, you need to seat your audience. A minor point of little interest? Not so! Seating arrangements can have a profound effect on the way that members of the audience respond to both the presenter and the presentation.

If it is up to you to arrange the seating at a presentation, you need to take account of two main factors:

■ audience size;
■ degree of interaction required between members of the audience and between the audience and the presenter.

the intimate brainstorm

For small groups and situations where you want the atmosphere to be reasonably open and a certain degree of discussion is expected, the appropriate seating arrangement will be the *Round table* or the *Open circle*:

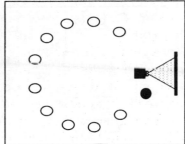

Round table layout   **Open circle layout**

The round table layout is appropriate if the audience will need a flat surface for drinks, to write notes, and so on. Where the main activity is to be a discussion, and will last for an hour or two at most, the open circle seating plan may be more effective in allowing communication between the participants.

> Note: These seating plans are unsuitable for groups of more than 20–24 people, and work best with groups of 12–15 people.

divided to conquer

Two of the most commonly used seating layouts for medium sized groups (say 20–30 people) are the *Open square* and the *Block*. They are easily adapted to fit wide rooms or narrow rooms and a variety of audience sizes with very little trouble:

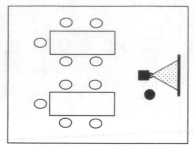

Open square layout   Block layout

These set-ups can be used for informal or formal presentations, as well as training sessions and any type of group which involves a certain degree of discussion, but which does not require the relative intimacy of the round table or the open circle.

The main weakness of the open square is that it reinforces the position of the presenter as the focus of attention, thus doing very little to encourage any team feeling.

For situations where a sense of team membership is an integral part of the event, you may prefer to use the block seating plan.

This seating arrangement creates individual groupings within the audience as a whole, and thereby encourages a team feeling and a greater willingness to interact as a group rather than just as individuals.

The most significant setback associated with this seating order is the fact that the people seated along the inside edge of each block need to turn sideways-on to the table in order to see the screen or flipchart. This might prove counter-productive if the audience is required to do a great deal of note-taking during the presentation, and in such cases the open square plan would be preferable.

come one, come all

For larger audiences (30 and over), there are three basic styles of seating plan that are suitable: the *Conference*, the *Restaurant* and the *Theatre*.

The main factors affecting your choice between these three plans are:

■ How long is the event?
■ Are the members of the audience required to take notes, or merely sit, look and listen?
■ How much room is available in relation to the size of the audience?

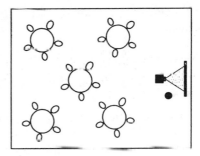

Conference layout   Restaurant layout

The conference layout allows a medium to high level of inter-action between audience and presenter, and is indicated where:

■ the event will last at least one full day;
■ the audience will need to take notes;
■ only low to medium interaction is required between members of the audience;
■ finding a large enough room to run the presentation with chairs and tables will not be a problem.

The restaurant style of seating is much favoured by some of the top business presenters, allowing a high level of interaction between the presenter and his audience (especially if the presenter uses the seating area as part of his own working space). It is often the only seating option available if the presentation is being run in a hotel which does not have specialized conference facilities.

It is also an arrangement which favours high interaction between members of the audience, if required, and can serve to enhance team identity (at the table-by-table level). Unfortunately, however, this same group identification can mean trouble for a presenter who is not used to working in this kind of situation and group activities can easily spill over into the presentation sessions.

Generally speaking, this layout is really only indicated where:

■ the event will *not* last for more than one full day;
■ the audience will need to do very little note-taking;
■ the presenter has well developed 'crowd control' abilities.

A further feature of this type of layout is the fact that it is inevitable that at least one or two people at each table (depending on the size of the tables) will need to spend most of their time facing towards the presentation area and away from the table. Many people find this arrangement somewhat unsettling and for that reason alone it is best avoided if possible. The only alternative is to have chairs round only the back half of the table – possibly an unacceptable waste of space where large numbers of people must be accommodated.

The last option – the theatre seating plan – is most suitable where:

■ the event will last for no more than one full day;
■ the audience will not need to take notes;

■ interaction between the audience and the presenter is not a key feature of the event;

■ no room can be found which is large enough to accommodate a presentation with both chairs and tables.

Theatre seating plan

This is another style of seating much favoured in hotel-based presentations. Unfortunately, hotel chairs are seldom of a sort designed for comfortable sitting over a prolonged period and this fact should be allowed for by providing correspondingly frequent comfort breaks.

if you want it done properly

One last word of warning before we leave the subject of seating arrangements:

■ *Never* assume that hotel staff will automatically know how to prepare a room for a presentation.

■ *Always* provide clear instructions in advance, preferably including a diagram of the required layout.

■ *Always* check the room layout for yourself on the day of the event *in plenty of time for it to be changed, if necessary.*

so many switches – so few hands

Only experience will teach you all the precautions that you need to take when doing a presentation away from home. Listed below are some of the most important pointers to setting up an effective presentation:

- When using electrical equipment always start by checking the location of the power outlets. Provide your own 'gang plug' and an extension lead to avoid difficulties caused by badly placed power outlets.

- Is everything set up correctly? Have you checked *every* piece of electrical equipment?

  If you're using any kind of projector, check that the screen and projector are correctly angled in relation to each other (the front of the projector and the screen should be parallel). If the projected image is larger on one side of the screen then pull that side of the screen forwards (towards the projector) until both sides of the image are equal.

  When using an OHP, make sure that you have room to stack used and unused foils in separate, easy-to-reach piles. Experiment to find an arrangement that feels comfortable, bearing in mind the need to stay clear of the screen area when changing foils.

- Check the heating/air conditioning controls. How accurate are they? Can they be easily reset? (In older buildings it may be difficult to control the heating on a room-by-room basis.)

  Keep the room slightly cool, even when full of people, in order to keep the members of the audience from getting so comfortable that they start to doze off.

- If the room/hall is large enough to require a sound system, is the microphone set at the right height (or are you going to be using a wire-less microphone)? In either case, make sure that you do a proper sound check *before* the event.

Few things are more unnerving than to start speaking and be interrupted by electronic feedback – the audible equivalent of sticking a knitting needle in one ear and out of the other. Feedback occurs when the output from one device (usually one of the speakers) is being picked up by the microphone, then sent back to the speaker, which feeds it to the microphone, and so on. (By the way, the signal from the speaker may not be loud enough to cause feedback until someone speaks into the microphone, so always do the sound check even if everything seems OK.)

■ If someone else is turning lights on and off for you during your presentation, make sure that the two of you run a last-minute rehearsal. If necessary, run several rehearsals until you are both sure that you understand what needs to be done.

■ If the lighting causes intrusive reflections, can you turn some lights off? If several lights are controlled by a single switch and you don't want to turn them all off, can you remove some of the bulbs to get the required result?

■ Check the audience area. Are there any broken seats? Get rid of them. Are there any soiled table covers? Have them replaced. If you are providing notepads, pens, handouts, soft drinks or water, and so on, is everything correctly set out?

■ Check your own area. Do you know what adjustments you will need to make (if any) after the previous speaker has finished?

Do you have a carafe of water and a glass on hand (see Chapter 14)?

If a lectern is provided, is it the right height? Does the light work (if any)?

■ Use clearly visible tape to hold down, and mark, any electric cables that could trip someone up.

the little things that count

Finally, having ensured that the presentation room is ready for business, there are just a few last little touches that will help to make your audience feel comfortable during the event:

- Where will tea and coffee be served *before* the presentation begins?

     Having the smell of good quality coffee wafting around is a well-known way of making a home more attractive to potential buyers. If you have the space, why not make the presentation room seem more welcoming by serving the first tea and coffee of the day at the back of the presentation room itself.

- Make sure that the staff responsible for clearing the crockery away won't interrupt the presentation. If possible, have refreshments served in another room.

- Now that smoking, and especially passive smoking, is a major social issue, you will need to designate specific smoking and non-smoking areas.

- Where appropriate, provide each delegate with a map of the venue and/or written instructions giving the routes between the presentation room and the main exit, the nearest fire exit (and assembly point), and the toilet facilities.

- Check the number of seats against the number of delegates. (If you aren't sure exactly how many seats will be needed, put out as many seats as you think you will need, and have some spare chairs stacked away in a corner.)

- If you're working with fixed seating, and there are clearly more seats than delegates, rope off the back row(s) of the audience area, and put out some 'RESERVED' notices.

question and answer sessions

why?

Here are just three of the many good reasons why you might want to accept questions from your audience:

- To create positive interaction between the members of the audience and yourself.
- By accepting audience questions *during* a presentation any misunderstandings can be cleared up on the spot.
- The questions that you get from the audience will give you a clearer idea of their level of understanding and areas of special interest, allowing you to fine tune your performance 'on the spot'.

when?

If allowing questions at any time has advantages, it also has certain disadvantages, from the presenter's point of view:

- You may get sidetracked by questions that are not strictly relevant.
- Questioners frequently ask about things that are of special concern to them as individuals, but that may not be of much interest to anyone else.
- It is very easy to lose track of time while answering questions so you end up having to rush through the last part of the presentation, in order to end on time.
- An unexpected or awkward question may disrupt the flow of the presentation and leave you looking ill-informed and unprofessional.
- In a 'worst case' scenario the questions could take up so much time that you cannot complete the presentation.

Daunting as the disadvantages may appear, there are relatively simple strategies for avoiding each and every one of them, which will, at the very least, contain the negative effects.

taking control of audience questions

One simple and very effective way of allowing questions while still keeping the presentation on track goes like this:

> I'll take any questions that call for *clarification* at any time during the presentation, but any questions which require *additional information*, or which relate to anything *not* directly covered in the presentation will be dealt with at the end of the session.

This approach assures the audience that you will cover all questions before the event is over, and also gives you the option of answering a question or putting it on hold as you see fit.

the three basic secrets of handling questions

secret no. 1

It is a natural reaction to start working out the answer to a question while the questioner is still speaking. Unfortunately, it is impossible to give your full attention to two separate lines of thought at the same time.

So, while a questioner is speaking *listen*. Cut a long-winded question short, by all means, but only start thinking about the answer *when the question is complete*.

secret no. 2

A common pitfall, when taking questions, occurs when only the presenter, the questioner and the first few rows of the audience know what question the presenter is answering. Fortunately there is a remarkably simple solution. Except in one special case (which will be covered in a later section) whenever you receive a question:

■ *rephrase* the question and then *repeat* it to the whole audience *before* you answer it;

■ then address your answer to the *whole* audience.

This action has three distinct advantages:

■ If the questioner does not correct your rephrased version of the question, you can be reasonably sure that you have both heard the question correctly *and* understood it.

■ Everyone in the audience knows what is going on.

■ You can think about five times faster than you can speak, so by repeating the question you give yourself valuable extra time in which to think about your answer.

secret no. 3

Avoid the trap of allowing yourself to be monopolized by just a handful of questioners.

Once you have accepted and repeated a question, aim to regulate your eye contact in the ratio of 20–25 per cent to the questioner, 75–80 per cent to the rest of the audience.

Looking at someone as you finish speaking is an implied cue for a reply. Only look at the questioner as you finish your answer *if you actually want the dialogue to continue.* Then you might also reinforce the message by asking something like: 'Does that answer your question?'

To *avoid* a follow-on question, simply direct your gaze to some other part of the room as you finish speaking, and indicate that you are ready to take a new question.

what to do when you don't know the answer

Be honest. Say 'I don't know' or, better still, 'I don't know, but I will find out'.

An even better response would be: 'I don't know, but I will find out by the end of the lunch break/tomorrow morning/etc.' And when you *say* you'll get the answer, make sure that you do.

an excuse is a loaded gun

Making excuses – for being late, for losing your place, for not knowing an answer or any other slip up – is a dangerous move. The excuse may be entirely true, but in the long run it solves nothing and excuses always tend to sound extremely feeble, even when they are true.

Dr Heckle

Dr Heckle 'questioners' don't really want to ask a question so much as make a provocative or disruptive statement. This is one time when you definitely *should not* repeat what has been put to you, unless the question/statement reflects to your benefit. Three easy actions will stop this kind of heckling:

- Ask the 'questioner' to identify herself. This breaks the audience's concentration, gives you extra time to prepare an answer, and starts to defuse the troublesome statement.
- Review the statement, looking for the underlying motive.
- Use your analysis of the statement to rephrase it as a question, so that the content is no longer antagonistic to your own position.

For example, the 'statement':

I can't see how you expect to increase the sales of Fanshaw's patent widgets when 50 per cent of our output is returned within six months!

Could be reworded as a question, thus:

OK, Joan has made a very good point here – how can we improve our production standards so as to increase our sales?

I think we should start by looking at the factors which have a direct influence on those standards

You don't have to distort a statement in order to turn it into a question, and if someone makes a statement so loaded that you'd rather not deal with it at all, simply defer it thus:

That's not really something I can give a straight 'yes' or 'no' answer to, but I'll be happy to discuss it with you in more detail when we break for coffee/lunch/tea.

Mr Jibe

A 'Mr Jibe' differs from a Dr Heckle by appearing to be siding with and assisting the presenter. Mr Jibe's questions usually start with a phrase such as: 'Isn't it true that...?'

The problem lies in the ambiguity of this opening phrase. The question may be an attempt to show off, or it may be a deliberate attempt to trap you into a mistake. It may even be a genuine question! In order to respond effectively to a 'Mr Jibe', whatever their motive, make sure that you adhere to the guidelines we've already discussed:

1. Wait until the question/statement is complete.
2. Reframe what has been said, using a lead-in phrase such as: 'If I've understood you correctly, you're saying [reframed statement]. Have I got that right?'
3. Be especially careful that you only answer Mr Jibe if you are sure of your facts. Otherwise, simply say something like, 'Well that's an interesting idea. I'll have to look into it when we take a break.'

No matter how confident Mr Jibe may sound, and no matter how plausible his comments, *never* assume that he knows what he is talking about.

beware the 'early bird'

An 'early bird' is a character who simply cannot wait to get at the 'worm' – the part of the presentation that she is particularly interested in. If the worm doesn't appear in what she considers to be a reasonable time, then she just has to get in there to try to rootle it out with a probing question.

The best way to deal with an early bird is to give her recognition and cut the question short all in one go, thus:

I do plan to cover that topic a little later on. Let me jot your question down so that I don't forget to answer it when we get to the appropriate point.

This response reassures the questioner that her enquiry has been taken seriously and will be addressed, but leaves no room for further discussion.

bones of contention

Some time or other you are bound to run into a 'hidden absolute' – a 'question' that starts with a phrase like:

Everyone knows that...
It's quite obvious that...

To take the sting out of this kind of question: *act dumb and ask for validation.* There is, of course, a right and a wrong way to do this, depending on whether you concentrate on the question or on the questioner. For example, let's suppose that Chris, a member of the audience, decides to question a course of action proposed by the presenter:

Chris: 'It must be obvious to everyone here that [this course of action] is bound to fail.'
Presenter: 'Hands up anyone who agrees with Chris.'

The hidden absolute here is the use of the word 'everyone'. In practice Chris may realize, as soon as he makes the comment, that it can, at most, only apply to everyone *except* the presenter, but the fact is that he said 'everybody'. And that's why a calm response is bound to win out. An absolute can only be true if it is *absolutely true.* Yet we already know that the presenter at least believes that the action will succeed, so the hidden absolute cannot be true.

Unfortunately this first reaction from the presenter has three important weaknesses:

1. The vote has now become a popularity contest.
2. Did *everyone* hear what Chris said?
3. The presenter has missed a golden opportunity to provide an alternative point of view.

A far better response might go like this:

> It has been suggested that the proposed action may not be completely successful. As the proposer of this action I can't agree with that, but what do other people think?
>
> Would the people who *don't* agree with the proposal like to raise their hands.

This second response:

1. Turns the original statement into a suggestion.
2. Demonstrates that the hidden absolute is incorrect, but without being confrontational.
3. Turns the vote into a 'sounding out' exercise, thereby removing the emotional charge.
4. Proposes the vote in negative terms. Since most people dislike agreeing to a negative proposition, this will minimize the support for the original statement.

Alternatively, the presenter could have asked a question such as: 'I wonder what makes you think that?' (An abrupt 'Why do you say that?' is definitely *not* the right way to tackle this kind of situation.)

Don't be afraid to hand the floor over to the speaker for a short while. When you think they've said enough simply thank them politely for their *opinion* and insist that time constraints mean that you must move on to the next question.

the good, the bad and the ugly

When you are adequately prepared, dealing with genuine questions should not present any serious problems. Even the odd 'difficult customer' can be handled using the following procedure:

step 1 – relax

Your natural reaction to a loud, contentious or rude 'question' from the audience may well be to tense up, with a dry throat and heart beating faster as extra adrenalin is pumped around your bloodstream. To counter these reactions, allow yourself to mentally withdraw for a moment and say to yourself: 'I am thinking about the fact that I am experiencing an emotional reaction.'

The process of thinking rationally about your feelings will enable you to view the situation more calmly, and to deal with it appropriately.

step 2 – be firm and polite

No matter how bad things look, be firm and polite. An audience will only support a presenter against a heckler as long as the presenter is *perceived* to be in control of himself.

step 3 – check the audience's body language

This will give you some important clues about what to do next:

■ If people are exchanging looks and settling back as though they know what's coming next, you are dealing with a regular heckler whose actions are seen by their colleagues as a form of entertainment. See Step 4, Option 1.

■ If people are paying more attention to the heckler than to you then they are probably in agreement with what is being said. See Step 4, Option 2.

■ If people look irritated and are watching you rather than the heckler, then they probably regard the heckler's comments as an unwelcome intrusion. In this case, they will tend to be on your side rather than the heckler's, and they will expect you to resolve the situation as soon as possible. See Step 4, Option 1.

■ When all else fails, see Step 4, Option 3.

step 4 – option 1

If you think that a heckler is simply sounding off, ask him what answer *he* would give. Remain calm and courteous until the heckler runs out of steam, or the other members of the audience begin to look bored, then bring the incident to a close with a polite but firm acknowledgement such as:

> Well, you clearly have very strong views on this matter, but I think we've gone as far as we can on this subject and I'm afraid I'm going to have to move on...

Maintain eye contact with the heckler for the first part of your response, but then make an obvious point of looking away – in search of further questions or comments – as you finish.

step 4 – option 2

When a questioner appears to have considerable support from other members of the audience, you will need to make a tactical decision as to the consequences of continuing the discussion.

Above all, be honest. The audience may not like your answer if it turns out that you cannot give the answer they want, but most people *can* see when they're being told the truth. If you stand your ground in a reasonable manner, it is more than likely that you will carry the day.

step 4 – option 3

If nothing else works, you may have to cut a heckler short. Make it clear that you feel that you have done all you can to satisfy the heckler's demands and can do no more.

If you have indeed played fair with the heckler, the other members of the audience will probably help to settle the matter for you by a show of mass disapproval.

in the seats of power

So far we've dealt with situations where the presenter is fielding questions single-handedly, either during or immediately after the presentation. From time to time, however, you may find that you are called upon to answer questions as a member of a panel. At first glance this may seem to be a situation where the chairman, as mediator between the audience and the members of the panel, will have a high degree of control. To an outsider, it might seem that members of the panel will simply come in with their individual contributions as and when they are called upon to do so. In reality things are a little more complicated than that, and the activities of each panel member tends to reflect their physical location in relation to the chairman.

In some cases, the seating arrangements may be made in advance so that individual panel members have no say as to where they will sit. On other occasions, however, it may be a question of taking your seat in order of entry on to the platform, or you may simply be allowed to sit wherever you chose. Even when the seating is pre-arranged, it may be possible to get the chairman's agreement to a slight re-arrangement, especially if no one else understands the significance of the various seating positions.

Many panel sessions have all of the members of the panel, plus the chairman, sitting in a straight line, as shown in this next illustration.

Chairman's Lines of Sight

The numbers in the circles on each side of the chairman indicate the relative influence of the person in that position (where the greater the number, the greater the influence). The only two seats of power on a straight line arrangement are the seats immediately next to the chairman. The two people in seats numbered 8 not only have the ability to pass notes and even speak directly to the chairman – they can also intercept messages passed to the chairman by other panel members should they wish to do so. The chairman's natural sight lines to the audience do not take in *any* of the panel members, and she must deliberately look to her left or right in order to be aware of any hand signals from members of the panel.

Where the panel is arranged in an open square (see next diagram), two further panel members are brought into the equation, because they intercept the sightlines between the chairman and the audience. This allows the people in the seats numbered 5 to catch the chairman's attention, even though they cannot communicate directly with her.

It follows from these two diagrams, that it is relatively easy (assuming that you have the choice of deciding where to sit) to decide whether to maximize or minimize your chance of taking an active part in the proceedings.

Some chairmen will have sufficient experience and expertise to ensure that everyone on the panel gets a fair crack of the whip. It may also turn out that your presentation, or at least your specialized knowledge, will attract a fair number of questions.

Chairman's Lines of Sight

In practice, however, chairmen are invariably selected on the basis of availability rather than skill, and it is far more likely that the part you play in the panel discussion will be dictated by the 'Chairman's Line of Sight' rules:

1. Your ability to control your part in a panel discussion is directly related to your ability to catch the chairman's attention, because...
2. The harder it is for the chairman to see you, the less likely it is that she will aim any questions in your direction.

personal presentation

here I stand

It is truly amazing how easy it is to become self-conscious about your body when you give your first few presentations. How should you stand or move, for example?

- No matter what you may have read or heard, moving around is no better, and no worse, than standing still.
- When standing still, aim to have your feet about shoulder width apart and keep your body square on to the audience and with your toes pointing slightly outwards. This stance is comfortable to maintain and indicates to the audience that you are relaxed and confident.
- Make sure that you are clearly visible to your audience, especially when you are saying something important. If you stand in front of a bright light, such as a well-lit window, your audience won't see much more than a black shape (which will literally be perceived as a negative image).

Here are some important 'posture pointers':

- Settling in one spot, leaning to one side.
  Hidden message: 'I'm bored and I'd rather be somewhere else.'
  Solution: When standing still, keep your weight evenly balanced and your hips level.
- Leaning over the top of the lectern.
  Hidden message: 'I'm too tired to stand up straight – or I just can't be bothered to do so.'
  Solution: When using a lectern, stand to one side rather than directly behind it.
- Sitting on the table provided for your notes, the OHP, etc.
  Hidden message: 'I don't have to make an effort here, because I'm more important than you.'
  Solution: No matter how relaxed you feel, stay standing!

In short, there is no ideal stance. Within reason, do whatever feels right for *you*. It is far more important that your verbal content, vocal style and body language should be congruent (all giving the same message) than whether you walk 3 metres or 3 kilometres while delivering your presentation.

you've got to hand it to him

The best way to use your hands during a presentation is to act as though you were in a normal conversation. If you usually wave your hands around in an animated fashion do the same thing (within reason) in a presentation. If you don't usually make much use of your hands when you're talking, that is fine, too. In short, if it doesn't feel comfortable don't do it – and don't worry about it, either. The members of your audience have no idea what to expect from you, and what they never see they won't miss.

tip:

If it feels natural to use your hands when talking, make sure that your gestures during a presentation are appropriate for the size of your audience. Thus the *more people* you are talking to, the *bigger* your hand and arm movements will need to be.

It may help you to decide what to do with your hands if you rehearse in front of the mirror or a close friend, to see what impression you will create.

Here are some poses you might want to avoid:

■ The 'stand at ease' stance – feet firmly planted and hands clasped behind your back. This looks stiff and overly formal. It is an 'authoritarian' stance, and will make it much harder to establish any degree of rapport with your audience.

■ Having your hands in your pockets looks unduly casual, or even sloppy. Having said that, if you find that your hands have wandered into your pockets:
  – Remove your hand(s) from your pocket(s) in a leisurely manner at a suitable moment (to point at something in a visual display, to turn a page of your notes, or whatever).
  – And for the men, if your hands find their way into your trouser pockets then above all, keep them still. If you fiddle with something in your pocket, no matter how innocent you may be, at least half of your audience are guaranteed to interpret your actions in the worst possible way!

■ Clasping your hands in front of you in the 'fig leaf' position looks rigid and uncomfortable and in English-speaking countries is generally recognized as a *defensive* posture, particularly for men. This stance will tend to set you apart from your audience and will lower your esteem in their eyes. It won't do much for your own self-confidence either.

■ Standing with your hands on your hips can look arrogant, affected or just plain silly, depending on your general physique. This was a favourite pose of the late Benito Mussolini, and look what happened to him.

■ Folding your arms over your stomach or chest can appear domineering in a large person, and is otherwise recognized as a defensive or divisive posture.

■ Rubbing your hands together in a 'washing' motion looks creepy, fussy and possibly dishonest.

just one look

The most basic link between any two people is *eye contact*. It is important, then, that you maintain more or less continuous eye contact with your audience. Two key elements which ensure dynamic eye contact with an audience are timing, and the Aura Effect.

As far as timing is concerned, you should look at any single person for no more than three or four seconds. Shift your gaze frequently, and preferably randomly (it is quite distracting to see an inexperienced presenter sweeping her gaze back and forth across an audience like some kind of human searchlight).

It isn't necessary to look at every single member of the audience in order to maintain effective contact. Indeed, the Aura Effect allows you to maintain rapport with whole groups of people rather than with isolated individuals. It works because our field of vision 'fans out' as it gets farther away.

The Aura Effect extends to the sides, in front of and behind the person the presenter is actually looking at. Thus, in the first illustration, when the presenter makes eye contact with one person near the front of the audience, at least four or five

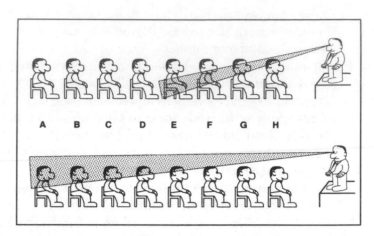

people are likely to think that he is looking straight at them. When the presenter turns his gaze towards the back of the audience, however, as many as 15 to 20 people are likely to believe that the presenter is looking at them, and them alone.

In general terms, then, you will want to maintain eye contact with your audience. But there are times when it can actually be beneficial if you deliberately *break* eye contact.

If, for example, you ask your audience to think something through for a few moments, you will get a better response if you lead the way by breaking eye contact and then mime being thoughtful until you are ready to continue.

To sum up, the overall image that you need to project for the best effect is one of relaxed control. This impression is most easily produced if it reflects what you really feel – when you know that you've done everything you can to ensure that the presentation goes well.

four keys to success

If this book were distilled into four key points they would be:

■ **Know your audience**
Who do you really need to talk to? What do you want them to hear? How do you want them to react? What will motivate them to respond in the desired manner?

■ **Keep it simple**
Language is an extremely inadequate medium for expressing any but the most simple ideas. So KISS (Keep It Short and Simple), and always talk to your audience as they are, not as you would like them to be.

■ **Keep to the point**
Don't underestimate your audience – but don't overestimate them, either. Be realistic. You only have a limited timeframe in which to tell your audience what they *need* to know, not everything that you know.

■ **Have confidence in yourself and in your message**
The audience will usually be on your side, at least at the start of the presentation. If you look confident and sound confident (but not arrogant) it is very probable that you will keep them on your side, even if you do make the odd mistake. You are far more likely to undermine that goodwill by being pompous or timid than by fluffing your lines, putting up the wrong slide or foil, or by running foul of the odd heckler.

style of speaking

Given that we develop our way of speaking over many years, can we really hope to develop a whole new vocal style?

Why not? All it takes is that you should want to improve your verbal skills. And the word *improve* really is crucial in this respect. Think of this as a progressive process, as an extension of your abilities.

Practise in front of a mirror and by talking into a tape recorder or a video camera. It doesn't really matter *what* you say at this point so much as *how* you say it. Find ways to make your voice more interesting, more expressive and more authoritative. As the ultimate test, read a column from your local telephone directory so that it sounds exciting, amusing or persuasive. You'll be amazed at how quickly you can begin to develop your vocal skills.

taking care of your voice

The Big Ben exercise (also known as the King Kong routine) is an easy yet effective way of deepening your voice and enhancing its flexibility. Make yourself comfortable, taking care that you are not constricting your chest or diaphragm in any way. Now, starting in your normal tone of voice, work your way down the scale singing 'ding, dong, bing, bong'. Keep going until you reach the lowest note that you can manage without straining your vocal cords. Then work your way up the scale until you reach the highest note that you can manage without strain. Finally, work your way back down the scale until you reach your normal tone of voice.

Repeat this exercise four or five times each session, one or two sessions per day, and you'll be amazed at the results. Your normal speaking voice will deepen; the range of notes that you can cover (without stress) will widen; and your voice will become more flexible, more varied and, above all, more interesting.

When you have acquired an interesting and flexible speaking voice, remember to keep it well exercised. During the colder months, take care that your throat is well protected when you go outside, and always take the appropriate kind of throat tablets or medicine if you detect any sign of soreness or irritation.

rehearsals

Your rehearsal(s) for a presentation should be part of the process of preparing your script.

Once you have drafted the outline of your script, put it on audio tape (videotape is even better) then run it through with the following thoughts in mind:

- ■ Does your presentation follow a clear sequence of ideas?
- ■ Have you aimed the material at the right level?
- ■ Have you included material that isn't strictly relevant?
- ■ Are you trying to cover too much information?
- ■ How and where can you use visual aids to clarify and enhance the basic presentation?
- ■ Are you presenting your material in an appropriate manner?

Armed with the answers to these questions, and any others which seem important to you, work your first draft into something more precise. When you think that you've developed a script that does what you want it to do, have another recorded rehearsal, asking yourself whether it really achieves the required result. It will also pay to take note of the *vocal interest* in your delivery (plus your *body language*, if you're doing a video recording).

When you first begin to give presentations you might also want to set the microphone a little way away from you so that you can learn to project your voice. There are two main points of difference between *projecting* your voice and *raising* your voice (the latter is technically referred to as shouting):

1a   To project your voice you must use your *diaphragm* to drive the air up through your throat and mouth.

1b   When you shout you use your *neck muscles* to do all the work.

2a   When you project your voice, you should find that you can talk as easily as if you were conversing with someone only a short distance away. Projecting your voice should not cause any kind of physical strain.

2b   When you shout, it *hurts*!

If you have trouble learning to project your voice correctly, you may find that it is worth paying a couple of visits to a professional voice coach or singing teacher.

Finally, when you feel that you've got things almost right – stop rehearsing. To give a really good performance you must have as much interest in your presentation as you want to see in your audience, and that's not very likely if you've already rehearsed it to death.

night and day, you are the one

The best state to be in just before you give a presentation is relaxed but alert. This may depend on whether you are a 'day person' or a 'night person'.

Day people find it easy to make an early start, but they tend to run out of steam later in the day. Night people, by contrast, may find it quite hard going to handle early morning sessions, and will be far more lively in the afternoon. If you are a night person and you have to give a presentation in the early morning, set the alarm at least a half-hour earlier than usual. This will give your body enough time to get into gear before you step into the spotlight.

For relaxation, on the other hand, you might like to consider listening to a tape of violin music by Mozart or one of the baroque composers (Vivaldi, Handel, etc), which is restful without causing drowsiness.

don't take it personally

Be aware that there never has been, and never will be, a *perfect* presentation. Whether any particular presentation goes well or not so well, there'll always be room for improvement.

Part of the learning process can be achieved through the use of evaluation sheets to get feedback from your audience. But beware – the responses that come back can range from absurd, through helpful, to the downright destructive. It shouldn't take you too long to realize that audience evaluations should be treated as either a learning opportunity or bin fodder, with not much in between. There are few (if any) experienced presenters who don't know *exactly* what is meant by the expression: 'You can never please *all* of the people *all* of the time.'

Incidentally, these evaluation sheets should be designed to elicit *comments* rather than *ratings*. Even then, the results can be pretty varied, as these pairs of review form comments show:

1a 'Pace too fast at times, and too in-depth in certain areas.'

1b 'Good structure, presentation and content.'

2a 'Pace generally too slow and notes do not add more detail to the lectures.'

2b 'Very detailed – lots to absorb in a day, but good notes to take away.'

3a 'Good clear concise material.'

3b 'Could do with better presentation material.'

4a '[the presenter] covered a tremendous volume of material quickly and lucidly.'

4b 'Disappointing – felt instructor's knowledge was too limited.'

Believe it or not, as they say, these comments (which are quoted in full) all refer to four different runnings of the same one-day presentation. On all four occasions the same person was giving the presentation, using the same materials. And yet, though each *pair* of comments were written on the same day, it is clear that audience perception varied quite radically as to the quality of both the presenter *and* the presentation.

In short, even when you exercise all of the communication skills you have at your command, there will always be someone in the audience who judges the event in the light of their own personal problems. It might be a hangover, a row with their husband/wife/partner/boss/underling, or any of the other little 'pricks and hurts that flesh is heir to'.

The trick, as explained in Chapter 4, is to know where to focus your attention. If you pay undue notice to the negative issues then presenting can become an onerous chore with very little reward. If you look *forward*, however, treating each new presentation as another opportunity to develop and hone your skills then presenting can be one of the most rewarding aspects of business life.

limbering up

Muscular tension can also affect your ability to speak easily and clearly. It is a good policy, therefore, to 'limber up' before you speak to get your body into the right state.

A little deep breathing is a good way to start. Make sure you get plenty of oxygen into your blood, but don't overdo it. Just three or four deep breaths will normally be sufficient to give you a bit of a lift. If you feel the least bit dizzy then stop immediately – you're probably hyperventilating and that won't help at all.

A safe way to loosen up your neck and shoulder muscles is the Chicken Peck.

Stand in a comfortable position, with your spine as straight as possible, next slowly push your chin out so that your whole head moves forward – making sure that your chin does not drop. Then bring your head back as far as it will go, still keeping your chin at the original angle. Do this 10 or 12 times in a steady rhythm, being careful not to strain the neck muscles.

If you do feel any tightness or discomfort in the muscles at the back of your neck, sit down and tilt your head back as far as it will comfortably go and count to 20. Then straighten your head and see how your neck feels. Repeat this as often as you need to – three or four repetitions will usually be sufficient to relieve all but the very worst neck ache.

desert mouth syndrome

Apart from forgetting what to say, nothing is worse than literally 'drying up' during a presentation. The first part of the remedy is to avoid anything that could cause 'desert mouth' syndrome. This includes salted snacks (crisps, peanuts, etc), smoking, and stimulants such as alcoholic drinks, coffee, tea and carbonated soft drinks, all of which can irritate the throat and cause 'desert mouth' syndrome.

One of the most effective ways of stimulating the production of saliva is to suck on a slice of lemon or to drink a little lemon juice. A far more practical solution is to have a supply of chilled (but definitely *not* iced) mineral water mixed with a touch of lemon or lime juice (experiment to find a balance that suits your palate). This makes a truly refreshing drink and an infallible antidote to 'desert mouth'.

a 'mighty, rushing wind'

And finally, you should also remember to avoid anything that is likely to cause flatulence or hiccups! Here, again, carbonated drinks are among the major villains, not to mention spicy foods. Do bear in mind, as well, that overeating *and* undereating can both cause embarrassing tummy rumbles during a presentation.

select bibliography

Argyle, M, Alkema F and Gilmour R (1970), 'The communication of friendly and hostile attitudes by verbal and non-verbal signals', *European Journal of Social Psychology*, 1, pp 385–402

Buzan, Tony (1989), *Use Your Head*, BBC Books, London (revised edn)

Buzan, Tony (1989) *Use Your Memory*, BBC Books, London (revised edn)

Honey, Peter and Mumford, Alan (1992), *The Manual of Learning Styles*, Peter Honey, Maidenhead (revised edn)*

Honey, Peter and Mumford, Alan (1986), *Using Your Learning Styles*, Peter Honey, Maidenhead*

Markham, Ursula (1989), *The Elements of Visualisation,* Element Books, Longmead

Mehrabian, A and Ferris, R (1967), 'Inference of attitudes from non-verbal communication in two channels', *The Journal of Counselling Psychology*, 31, pp 248–52

Miller, George A (1956), 'The magical seven, plus or minus two: some limits on our capacity for processing information', *Psychological Review*, No 63, pp 81–97

O'Connor, Joseph and Seymour, John (1993), *Introducing Neuro-Lingusitic Programming*, Aquarian/Thorson, London, (revised 2nd edn)

Ostrander, Sheila and Schroeder, Lynn with Ostrander, Nancy (1981), *Super Learning*, Sphere Books, London

Pease, Allan (1992), *Body Language*, Sheldon Press, London (new edn)

Rose, Colin (1985), *Accelerated Learning*, Accelerated Learning Systems, Aylesbury

---

* These two books are published privately and are available directly from Peter Honey, Ardingly House, 10 Linden Avenue, Maidenhead, Berkshire, England SL6 6HB.